Memoir of a Skipjack

BY

RANDOLPH GEORGE

ISBN 978-1-62806-124-6 (print | paperback)

Library of Congress Control Number 2017934696

Published by Salt Water Media
29 Broad Street, Suite 104
Berlin, MD 21811
www.saltwatermedia.com

Acknowledgments

In researching this book, I had the good fortune to meet and talk with several members of the Wingate and Tilghman Island communities, and with former owners of *Martha Lewis*. Without their generous sharing of time and information, none of this would have been possible. In the fall of 1993 and in several visits and conversations thereafter, I spoke with:

Dan Dize

Dave Faulkner

Mary Parks Harding (MPH in the family tree)

Gail Sterling Joubert (GSJ in the family tree)

Anna A. Lewis Sayers

Katherine "Kitty" Lewis (KL in the family tree)

Osylee Lewis

Calvert "Cody" Parks

Dorothy Ann Lewis Shortall (DL in the family tree)

Deenie and Troy Tyler

Lucille Parks Sterling (LS in the family tree)

Lemuel Lewis, Sr.

William "Snooks" Windsor

I am also indebted to Fred Hecklinger and Allen and Liz Rawl for their dedication and expertise, and to Maureen McNeill for her editorial prowess and encouragement.

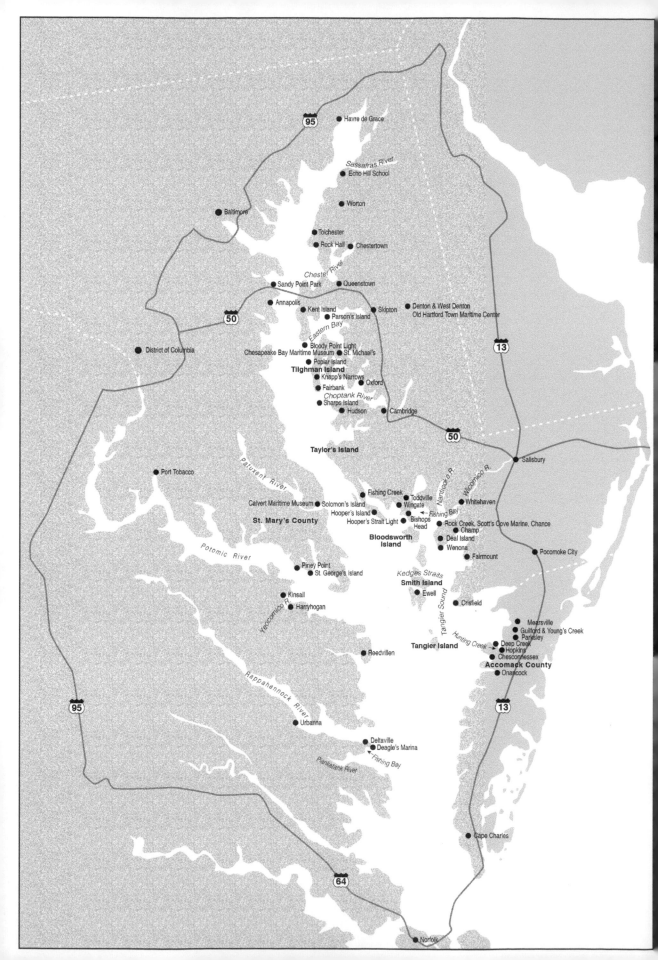

Table of Contents

Coming home. Kent Narrows. September 1993

Introduction

A generation ago the Chesapeake Bay was still giving up modest harvests of seafood, though nothing like the massive volumes of fishes, crustaceans, and shellfish of the 1800s, when there seemed no limit to nature's bounty. In small towns along hundreds of miles of the vast Chesapeake, men and boys in boats set out year after year to collect all they could from the waters that sustained them. Chesapeake literature abounds with tales – occasionally filtered through a veil of myth – of mighty catches and grinding labor, of pirates and murder, of storms and destruction and of heroic deeds.

The earliest watermen had an independent existence, bound only by the laws of nature, family, friendships and admonitions heard on Sundays. Driven by far-off markets in Baltimore and Philadelphia, they competed to out-work their brethren through shrewdness and guile, all the while plying the skills of their forebears with a fraternal identity which set them apart from others.

Though only one of the products of the Bay, the oyster is a resource upon which many thousands of persons have depended for generations. The swampy town of Crisfield, Maryland, for example, literally was raised on mounds of bivalves off-loaded at her docks. Boats, wagons and, eventually, train cars full of oysters flowed from such collection points to seafood purveyors throughout the entire eastern United States.

Slowly the great Bay grew tired. In the middle of the 20th Century parasitic diseases plagued the oyster population and by the 1980s only 1% of its historical numbers survived. With the loss of these natural filters and with a human population that dumped progressively more waste into the Bay, the waterman's work and history began to wane. There were fewer oysters, more people, and the oyster fleets gradually dwindled. As tongers and dredgers competed for the diminishing fishing grounds, the efficiency of dredgers gave them an advantage, and laws were passed to limit their dredging areas and catches. Schooners, bugeyes and skipjacks were run up into the marshes and abandoned.

Blue crab fisheries suffered as well, and rockfish, a favorite type of striped bass, approached extinction until a moratorium on their harvest brought them back from the brink.

When the world makes us homesick for a less complicated time, or for greater commonality and community, some of us look to history for safe harbors. Today, the skipjack era is slowly passing, but what remains of it is held dear by those who call the Chesapeake home. Few are those without memory, vicarious or real, of the traditions that make their region unique, special and seemingly favored.

This book is written mainly about one boat, but one which survives as a living evidence of an important era. She is one of the few remaining fishing boats to work under sail in the U.S. and, as such, serves as a valued anchor to our past.

She takes us back to a time when there was still a robust oyster industry and an expectation that a living could be eked from the Chesapeake, when those with determination could support a living like the one their fathers perpetuated for centuries. She takes us back to small waterside hamlets, where oystermen caulked, hammered and painted, repairing the boats that would carry them in the fall to the rock piles and reefs that had always given up deck-loads of oysters.

Chapter 1

Saving a Skipjack

In 1993 I bought a skipjack.

There probably are not many folks in the world who even know what that means, but it's a story worth telling. The skipjack at the center of this tale is a boat, a very special boat, unique in time and place. When I first saw her, she was docked at a marina on Tilghman Island in Talbot County, on the Eastern Shore of Maryland. She was a little rough around the edges, but, like an aging actress, she carried herself with elegance and mystery. I thought she was beautiful.

Finding the boat was not an accident. I was looking for her. The seeds for this story clearly began years before when I first found myself on the shores of the Chesapeake Bay. During most of the 1970s I was immersed in a neurosurgical residency program at Johns Hopkins Hospital. Though the training was nearly all-consuming, it allowed some precious time away from the hospital for me to discover my surroundings, the lore of the Bay and, especially, the city of Baltimore.

As a port city, Baltimore owes much of its history and commerce to the Bay and its connection to the sea. Her harbor was home to trading and fighting vessels of every stripe. America's clipper ships sailed from here in the Golden Age of Sail. The Star Spangled Banner flew over her fort when a young nation had to reassert its independence. Though we now look back upon it through a nostalgic lens, her once hard-scrabble waterfront was home to countless merchants, hucksters, watermen and sailors, to saloons and impressment gangs.

But the city grew and a polyglot mix of immigrants imbued her with their energy and character. Slowly the waterside warehouses and wharfs, teeming with tall-masted ships, passed away. Now they are almost forgotten amid the high-rise opulence that has replaced them.

Soon after I finished my course at Hopkins, and a stint at Portsmouth Naval Hospital, in Virginia, my profession took me away from the mid-Atlantic to a career in Birmingham, Alabama. The Bay remained a draw, however, and when I began to plan retirement, it was the Bay which drew me back. In 1986 I bought an old colonial home in Somerset County on Maryland's Eastern Shore and began to lay down roots.

The Eastern Shore of Maryland, lying between the Chesapeake and the Atlantic, is near the epicenter of some of America's earliest recorded history, including its rich maritime heritage. Here live the watermen who work the Bay, hauling in crabs in summer and oysters in winter. Here live the descendents of boat builders who supplied the watermen their tools of commerce for generations.

As it happens, my brother-in-law was a boat builder, and one with impressive credentials. Allen Rawl started out working on the construction of the replica clipper ship *Pride of Baltimore*. After that, he participated in the restoration of the 1906 skipjack *Minnie V.* and in the building of her facsimile *Anna McGarvey*. Among his many other projects, he built

Anna McGarvey. Crisfield, MD. July 1993.

the full-scale representations of the immigrant ships *Susan Constant* at Jamestown, Virginia, and *Kalmar Nyckel* at Wilmington, Delaware.

One day Allen and I drove down to Crisfield at the lower end of Somerset County to see a skipjack we heard was there. We found her at the dock behind the Maritime Museum. She seemed to be dying. She had broken spars, a crumbling deck, with a pump continuously emptying her bilge. "Such a shame," we thought, such a poignant example of a passing era. We climbed aboard and stepped gingerly over rotten planks and fallen rigging. At first, Allen was analytical, but then he became visibly curious and, finally, surprised. "I can't believe it! This is *Anna Mc-Garvey!*" He recognized a boat that he had helped to build with his own hands now sadly neglected and allowed to decay. Both of us felt a sense of nostalgia and loss.

Over the next several months I returned to the Shore, and set out with Allen to discover what was left of the once-mighty skipjack fleet. We traveled all over the Eastern Shore of Maryland, following leads and photographing nearly every skipjack that still existed. These are presented in Appendix B.

We found a total of 2 bugeyes, which are two-masted oyster boats, and 52 single-masted skipjacks. Of the latter, 5 had been built as yachts. Six were out of commission, but were preserved on land under cover or in museums. Twelve were totally dead and 32 were either working or at least able to float.

In the process, my regard for skipjacks grew from mere curiosity into mission. Maybe it came from not wanting to watch something die, to hold on to something of worth, while there was still time. Anyway, one night, over beers, we decided to save one skipjack, to keep it from its likely fate of rotting in the mud in some creek along the Bay. And so we decided to find one that was in trouble, but not too far gone to repair.

There were 5 for sale in 1993, and Allen examined each one, crawling below decks, poking planks and timbers with his pen knife, looking for decay. Some were too far deteriorated, some had inflated prices, but one seemed a likely candidate. Its price tag was $30,000. It had mild-to-moderate rot, but was definitely salvageable. In due course we found that our first impression of her was a bit too rosy, but we couldn't know that until her planking came off and we saw below the surface. Her name was

Martha Lewis. Over the next several years we grew to know her well. She shared with us a rich lore from her past and introduced us to the people who had created her and depended on her for a living.

The book I ultimately decided to write is a record of what Allen and I discovered in refurbishing *Martha Lewis*. I intend it as a document, a study, a memoir. I began to write it over twenty years ago and, for me, the story has not diminished over time.

Skipjacks are a uniquely Chesapeake Bay invention and are all that remain of America's commercial fishing vessels powered by sail. They evolved prior to the 1890s from earlier forms, especially the unframed Chesapeake Bay crabbing skiff. They were an answer to shallow waters, the need for simple construction, and to the development of a most efficient tool for harvesting oysters, the large rake known as the dredge. These boats had to be powerful, yet smartly maneuverable.

Their design was a product of a constantly evolving boat-building tradition that continues to this day. In 1900 approximately 700 oyster dredgers of various types worked the Bay, accompanied by many hundreds of smaller boats used for scraping and hand tonging. This armada included log canoes, brogans, pungy schooners, skiffs, bugeyes, sloops and skipjacks. Today hand- and patent tongers greatly outnumber dredge boats, which are now only a handful of active skipjacks.

Skipjacks are always made of wood, although some captains have recently tried to preserve them by coating their hulls with plastic. For a work boat, their form is enchantingly elegant, not least because of their long clipper bows. A few of the older vessels have round bottoms with fore-and-aft planking, but the vast majority have bottoms planked either at right angles to the keel or chevroned with the boards angled aft from keel to the chine. A "hard chine" is the typical sharp-angled edge between a skipjack's bottom and sides. The boats are called dead-rise bateaux because their bottoms are not quite flat, but are angled in a broad V upward from the keel.

The boats are built for stability, with wide beams that measure about one third the length of the deck. They have raked straight stems, slightly raked sterns, and usually a square transom, square at the waterline and elliptical at the deck. Historically, the length on deck has varied widely from 27' to 60'. There is only a single deck, called a flush deck, though it sheers slightly upward from stern to stem. The freeboard at midship is deliberately – and uniquely – low. Nearly all skipjacks are decorated with carved and painted trailboards at the bow, sporting scrolls and shields and the name of the boat. Some vessels have figureheads, often carved eagles.

Bugeyes have two masts and are called three-sail bateaux, but skipjacks have one tall mast. They carry stout bowsprits and long booms. All have centerboards and can be considered centerboard sloops. The bowsprit on a skipjack is square aft and round near the tip. Some are triangular, providing a flat surface to stand on while tending the head sail. The rudder posts are slanted or vertical. There is usually a Samson post and windlass at the heel of the bowsprit. The mast height is roughly the length of the boat on deck plus its width or beam. The boom measures approximately the same length as the boat on deck. The mast is positioned at a variably raked angle aft and has double or triple shrouds.

The large mainsail, called a "leg-o'-mutton" mainsail because of its nearly isosceles shape, is laced to the boom and is held to the mast by oaken hoops. A few skipjack captains rig their mainsails with a wooden sprit, called a club, lashed to the luff of the head of the sail to increase its height above the mast. The large jib is tacked to the end of the bowsprit and usually has another club on its aft foot to which the sheets are attached. Rigging includes a forestay, jib stay and a topping lift from the end of the boom. "Lazy-jack" lines restrain the mainsail and jib during furling.

Skipjacks typically carry one captain and a 5-man crew. On today's skipjacks, the skipper stands either before or alongside the wheel, since the gearbox fills the space between wheel and transom. The wheel is mounted a short distance behind the boat's cabin, called the trunk cabin, where a ladder leads down into a living space in the hold. Atop the entrance to the cabin, a doghouse adds just enough height for ease of access. Forward of the cabin is a pair of winders for cables that raise the dredges, powered originally by hand, but then for many decades by a gasoline or diesel engine. Forward of the winders a short section of deck separates them from a large square hatch leading to the forward hold just behind the mast.

In the early 20th Century a small motorized barge, called the push boat or yawl boat, was added to the vessel's equipment. This odd adaptation provides an outboard engine carried in a small unmanned skiff, behind the skipjack's stern. When not in use, this little boat hangs athwartships from davits. When needed for propulsion or steering, it is lowered into the water and its bow is securely tucked into a padded "jig" on the skipjack's transom. Lines from the skiff's quarters are tended with electric winches on each of the larger boat's davits, though for many years this work was done entirely by hand. A second pair of lines is secured midship on the pushboat and, with block and tackle, is used to raise and lower its bow and stern separately. This requires a choreographed effort by captain and crew to avoid swamping, especially in heavy weather.

Fishing laws prohibited the use of push boats for dredging until 1967 when they were first allowed for dredging on Mondays and Tuesdays during oyster season (today from November 1 to March 15). The other days were reserved for working only with sail.

From the late 1880s through the first half of the 20th Century skipjacks became a dominant and essential workboat. They were relatively inexpensive to build and they were produced by skilled carpenters all along the Eastern Shore of the Bay in Maryland and Virginia, and on the southern Western Shore south of the Potomac. A few were even built in North Carolina. Most coastal harbor towns hosted skipjacks in the heyday of dredging under sail. Depending on available materials, builders' experience, individual whims and local traditions, their construction varied widely. All were built to maximize the ratio of efficiency to cost in the business of collecting oysters. Yet, because they were utilitarian, they were ultimately disposable. The boats were made of local loblolly pine, which could be patched and repaired for several years before fungus and rot caused their owners to run them up into the marshes to die. This notwithstanding, they became the quintessential working boat of the Chesapeake and, as such, came to be imbued with the area's history, its personality and its pride. They have been Maryland's official "state boat" since 1985.

Reconstructing a skipjack requires considerable planning, including locating materials, talent and funding. I decided to pay for the project myself and Allen knew all we needed about the rest. His boat building contacts included shipwrights and lumber suppliers, blacksmiths and rope merchants, riggers and caulkers. After a flurry of letters and phone calls, we found a new home port and a place to build a boatyard at Havre de Grace, Maryland, at the head of the Chesapeake Bay. The town loaned us property near the Concord Point Lighthouse while the local maritime museum and boat school invested enthusiastic crews of volunteers.

Capt. Michael Rawl
at helm of *Martha Lewis*.
September 1993.

Martha Lewis introduced herself to us in stages. As soon as we had secured her new home, our group of boat hands brought her up the Bay from Tilghman in September. Our skipper was Michael Rawl, Allen's son, an experienced East Coast boat captain. The boat was new to all of us. It would take time to learn her peculiarities and how to handle her. The push boat engine needed repairs as soon as we got out of Dogwood Harbor. The weather was rainy and cold, but once we were in open bay she filled her sails and charged through the water, making seven knots. As she heeled, and the rush of water flowed over her lee rail, we realized that we had taken charge of a large, spirited creature requiring close attention.

No one was aware or particularly concerned that the boom previously had been spliced about three-quarters aft of the jaws. The breeze freshened to around 25 knots and we were surprised when this splice point gave way.

I was standing at the starboard shrouds when I heard the "crack" and saw the forward end of the boom fly several feet up the mast. Astern, the middle of the boom crashed onto the starboard cabin top, missing our captain by inches. We stowed the sails and went back to using the push boat.

That night we motored into Tolchester harbor in the rain, anchored and slept on board. Skipjack crew berths are in the forward hold and

Martha Lewis under sail from Tilghman to Havre de Grace.
September 1993. Courtesy Elizabeth Rawl.

provide little in the way of comfort. The cabin is warmer, but only slightly more commodious, with single hard bunks on either side and one behind the ladder. The following morning, at daybreak, we set out for Havre de Grace. We had a small stove and made a breakfast of coffee, eggs and bacon as we continued up the Bay.

I can still recall the smells of that day and others like it...the smells of the Bay, of the water in the bilge, of tar and mildew, of bacon, of sweat and fumes from the push boat engine.

I have sailed on *Martha Lewis* many times since then, but the memories are always the same, laced with exhilaration and an awareness of adventure.

Since at least the 1920s, dredge boat captains reserved special days in early September, just prior to the oyster season, for racing their boats. World War II interrupted these competitions, but despite a diminishing dredging fleet, the tradition has held. It serves as additional incentive for captains to finish their summer repairs and compete with their fellow watermen. Several hundred dollars in prize money awaits the wily captain and crew who can claim bragging rights over the rest of the fleet. For many years races were held in late October at Sandy Point, near the Bay Bridge, during Chesapeake Appreciation Days, but other venues have included Cambridge, Tilghman Island, Solomon's Island and, most enduringly, Deal Island.

Considering the cost of fuel required for travel to the race site, a surprising number of skipjacks show up. They raft up two and three deep in the host harbor and watermen clamber across each others' decks as they joke and jibe with their fellow competitors. None is a stranger, but still there is a wary camaraderie as the captains gather for instructions at the pre-race meeting on shore.

Family and friends then climb aboard, throw off dock lines, lower the push boats and motor out to the starting line in the channel. Push boats are hoisted and sails are set. In recent years non-working dredge boats are allowed in the races and are towed out to the race course. The scene is surprisingly majestic as old, patched sails pass fresh, white canvas, while the captains jockey for position to be first across the line. The competition is already fierce before the starting gun, resulting in occasional collisions, bowsprits fouling the rigging of other boats, yelling and swearing and a general demonstration of fierce determination.

I have sailed on winning and losing races on *Martha Lewis* and count them among some of my fondest memories. Race day is something of a reunion of kindred spirits, a time to remind us of all the reasons we want to preserve traditions.

As I write this, I am reminded of a race day at Deal Island when we all puzzled at Captain Art Daniels on *City of Crisfield*. We watched as he sailed far afield from us, in nearly the opposite direction from the buoy which was our turning mark. He nearly disappeared. Then he tacked onto a reach and barreled down on the mark, passing all the rest to win the race. Besides being an expert sailor, he knew his home waters, their depths, their currents and their tides – their history.

As soon as Allen and his crew began their serious work on restoring *Martha Lewis*, I set out to find her former owners. Fortunately, they were still available to tell their stories, were generous with their time and were eager to record their memories. This book is dedicated to them.

Chapter 2

Bronza's Boatyard

For many years the small town of Wingate, on the southern peninsular tip of Dorchester County, Maryland, was in relative isolation. The Old Bay Line steamship company had a wharf on a small island at the end of Wingate Point Road, about a mile and a half west of town. Most travel across the Bay was to Baltimore, until the landing was closed sometime after the First World War. Then transportation was by car or truck two hours north to Grasonville in Queen Anne County. From there the car ferry sailed to Baltimore. In 1952 the Chesapeake Bay Bridge from Kent Island to Sandy Point opened the Eastern Shore of Maryland, Virginia, and Delaware to road traffic.

Wingate is a small community on the Honga River that clings to a largely agricultural and fishing existence. Scattered nearby are the hamlets of Andrews, Bishop's Head, Lakesville, Crapo (originally Woodland-town), Crocheron and Toddville. Each was founded by some of the first English settlers to come to America. In the days when transportation was by water, the small Wingate harbor on Hearns Cove was a haven; and when oyster populations were huge, it was home to many dozens of fishing vessels and the waterman that used them. Other European immigrants populated the neighboring islands called Bloodsworth, Hooper's, Pone (Adams), Holland and Taylor's. Before these islands began to disappear beneath the waters of the Chesapeake Bay, they were home to numerous communities that wrested an existence from fishing, crabbing, oystering and the building of boats. Family names in these parts included Bloodsworth, Windsor, Dean, Lewis, Todd and Parks.

Bronza Malone Parks came into the world on January 20, 1900, in Wingate. His father and grandfather were oyster dredgers and his maternal grandfather built boats. From age 16 to 23 Bronza worked on the

Wingate harbor. 1950s. Courtesy of Mary Parks Harding.

water and at some point he was half owner in a skipjack. The record
of his marriage date with Katie Thelma Lewis is not definite, but we
do know that he went into business in a crab house with Katie's brother William "Willie" Lewis from about 1918 until 1920. They called the
business Lewis and Parks. When it burned down, they did not rebuild
it. Willie returned to the water and Bronza ("Bronzie") began building
boats.

He built his first several boats in customer's yards, before he set
up his own boatyard. His daughter Mary remembers that he built the
dovetail work boat, *Dorothy Lee*, in Theodore Woodland's yard at Bishop's
Head, just south of Wingate, in 1933. This boat was a Hooper's Island
launch, also called a draketail, ducktail or "torpedo stern." It was used
with an inboard gasoline engine for running crab trotlines. Bronza built
it during the Depression, and charged $350.

Bronza and Katie had five children, all girls: Irene, Lucille, Martha,
Mary and Joyce. Mary remembers going with her father into the woods
to look for straight pines suitable for masts. She remembers her early life

in Wingate as "utopian." Her recollections and those of several neighbors are the source of most of what we know about the most productive enterprise in Wingate history. All agree that the little community, with its Methodist Church and its one-room schoolhouse, seemed to have a shared admiration for decency. It was very religious, tightly-knit, and uncommonly cooperative.

The boat shed and yards were set up near the house on Parks Road. Using his family heritage, the advice of older boat builders and his innate ambition, Bronza perfected his craft from the 1920s until his untimely death in 1958. He produced bay craft of all sorts, including crabbing and fishing vessels, and he was much admired for the excellence of his pleasure yachts and cruising boats. In all, his yard and shop produced more than 400 vessels in his career.

In 1993, just after I purchased *Martha Lewis*, I traveled to Wingate to meet with Osylee Lewis, Calvert Parks and Oneal Dean. Osylee's father had entrusted Bronzie to build *Martha Lewis* in 1954; Calvert was Bronza's nephew and had worked in the boatyard, including the time when *Martha Lewis* was being built. Oneal Dean worked in the yard, as well. All three agreed that Bronza never worked from blueprints. He may have made sketches, but directed his yard crew without written instructions.

Calvert, born in 1929, started working for Bronza when he was a 13 years old and said his employer would pay him $5 a week, and sometimes gave him a tool as further enticement. He eventually earned $20 a week working in the boat yard.

Oneal "Neal" Dean started working for Bronza when he was 16 and remembered that the work was hard. Before electricity came to Wingate they worked entirely with hand tools, and did so for 10 hours a day, 6 days a week.

Bronza insisted on perfection. When things were not done exactly, he would have the work torn out, regardless of the cost. He insisted on smooth lines and surfaces. Osylee recalled that Bronza sometimes could be irritable and gruff, but had a reputation of always being fair. Mary Harding, Bronza's daughter, says that he also had a playful, even boyish side. She remembers her father, boat builder, manager, leading businessman in the community, tossing his hat on the floor and turning cartwheels.

The lack of blueprints did not mean that Bronza lacked a clear idea of how each detail should be rendered. He was uncannily correct in estimates of lengths and shapes without a ruler. He always insisted that building matters were "right or wrong."

Calvert had to learn about this the hard way. As long as Bronza was on hand to guide his workers, all went as it should. But one day Bronza had to be away from the boatyard and "told us not to do nothin' 'til he got back. 'I want that stern real purty, ya know.' I was workin' with Ralph (Ralph Ruark, who later became Bronza's son-in-law) and I swear I didn' mean to say it, but I said, 'ya gotta be goin' ta work, don't ya, Ralph.' He says, 'You know I always go to work. He told us not to do nothing,' 'But we gotta get the stern done,' I says, and he said 'alright then.'" So they got to work and Bronza didn't come back for a long time. Calvert said, "so here he come down there out the barn, sorta wobblin', ya know how he would." (Bronza's daughter, Mary, said he walked with a kind of limp.) "He looked at that stern and made us take it all down. He'd get this stuff in his head, ya know. If he'd drawn it on paper, a fella would know."

Calvert, who was always called Cody (pronounced Cotty), interrupted a boat-building career in the 1940s to dredge for oysters. He said that the watermen were just coming out of the Great Depression and could make a good living dredging. Cody eventually went to work in Jim Richardson's boat yard on LeCompte Bay near Cambridge. He said Richardson always used blueprints, but "couldn't build a boat like Bronza."

As Bronza's business prospered, he hired more Wingate hands in the boatyard. Osylee Lewis remembered that Tom Dean, Lindy Moore, Oneal Dean, Oneal Jones, Bobby Parks, Bobby Powley, Cody Parks and, probably Lowell "Coosey" Moore worked in Bronza's yard. Oneal Windsor and his brother "Snooks" Windsor (William Hudson Windsor), Reuben Murphy and Eddie Abbott also worked there. Mary Parks Harding said he always had work for the young men of the town, and that most young men in Wingate worked for her father at one time or another. She remembered fondly that, if there was nothing for them to do, Bronza would throw nails around the yard when he finished up at night, so that they would have something to do the next day. On Sundays he would give one of the

Crew taking a break at Parks Boatyard. Tom Dean on mandolin, F. Oneal
Dean on guitar, and Ralph Ruark on fiddle. 1950s Wingate.
Courtesy of Mary Parks Harding.

Bronza Parks and finished pleasure boat.
Courtesy of Mary Parks Harding.

boys a quarter to wash his Model A Ford.

At its busiest, B. M. Parks Boat Builders had 13 boats under construction at the same time, with 27 workers. In the 1940s Bronza was selling 42' work boats for $650. In the mid-1950s he was turning out 25 boats a year.

Osylee Lewis tells a story about Bronzie and his brother Orville. "Orville asked Bronzie, 'Now Buddy (he called 'm Buddy), why don't you build a good work boat for me?' So Bronza had a standard price he gave to Orville. Orville was real shrewd, y' know; he'd go to scratchin' hisself, whinin' and gruntin.' He said, 'My God, Bronzie, that's a terrible price! You oughta be able to do it cheaper for me." Bronza says, 'Why's that, brother?,' Orville says, 'Because I'm your brother.' And Bronza says, 'Well, in that case, you ought to give me a little bit more, 'cause I'm your brother.'"

In 1954 the Chesapeake Bay was visited by a ferocious storm, Hurricane Hazel. At Wingate the water rushed into the town and boats were tossed inland. Mary Parks Harding recalled that one boat washed as far as their porch on Parks Lane. Osylee Lewis's workboat, named *Anna Arlene* after his daughter, ended up in the woods. The National Guard spent several days in Wingate, aiding with the clean-up, and the Army Corps of Engineers helped to retrieve all the boats and return them to the water. Apparently none of the boats was completely destroyed.

The storm struck in the middle of a decade when there were still enough oysters to make dredging profitable, even though disease and overfishing had already begun to deplete the fishery. In the spring of 1955 Bronza's boatyard was particularly busy, with boats under construction in the shop and three skipjacks just begun out back.

The skipjack keels were begun in succession in the boat house, and were built "upside-down with the keelson on top". The keels, which locals called keelsons, were held up by an overhead beam. When the boats were sufficiently framed, Bronza blew a siren to gather the crew, and, using "winches, blocks, and falls", they turned them over. They hauled them to the yard behind the boathouse, cribbed them, and began planking.

The yard was a beehive of activity, with the crews sawing and planing, measuring and nailing. The three boats were built nearly the same,

Bronza Parks and Jim Lewis, Jr. in boatyard. October 1955.
Courtesy of Mary Parks Harding.

Crew with skipjack mast at Parks boatyard. 1955.
Courtesy of Mary Parks Harding.

Left to right: *Lady Katie*, *Martha Lewis*, and *Rosie Parks* under construction. 1955. Courtesy of Mary Parks Harding.

Jim Lewis in Parks boatyard, splicing lines for *Martha Lewis*. October 1955. Courtesy of Mary Parks Harding.

with only slight variations. James Lewis and Orville Parks commissioned two of them and another man, whose name has been forgotten, commissioned the third. James Lewis named his *Martha Lewis*, after his mother, and Orville called his *Rosie Parks*, after his mother. The man who ordered the third boat did not give it a name, because he died during its construction. Bronza kept this third boat as his own. Mary Parks Harding, who had four sisters, tells of asking her father to name the skipjack for her, his "best girl." She says her father smiled and told her he had only one best girl. He named the skipjack *Lady Katie*, for his wife. *Martha Lewis* was built between the other two boats.

Cody remembered that the three skipjacks were built "every bit of them of pitch pine. Bronzie used the rule that the mast was length plus width, so the *Rosie Parks* had a mast about 65' tall. I imagine the other two were about the same. These boats were fast, the best skipjacks there was. *Rosie Parks* was the fastest. Bronzie kept the mast straight... that was a definite for drudgin'. A lot of them boys let the masts get out of hand, with a curve. The *Collier* was one. It would drown ya t' drudge it, 'cause to pull and drudge it, y' had to have a 20-mile breeze. When we plumbed the mast up, it worked very well. It didn't take much to move the step four or so inches, then wedge it, and you'd get 6' on top."

By October of that same year, 1955, the boats were ready to launch. Bronza devised a cradle out of timbers and four large wheels to carry them the quarter-mile to the harbor. In earlier years he used a Ford truck to haul his boats to the water, but now he used a tractor. Each boat took a day to move.

Word of the three skipjacks reached a member of Delaware's prominent du Pont family, a great-great grandson of the founder of the du Pont industries. Irénée du Pont drove down to Wingate and asked Bronza to build another skipjack, just like the others, but with a long cabin for cruising. Bronza agreed and built her in front of the boathouse. She was launched the following year, in June, 1956. Du Pont named her *Barbara Batchelder* and sailed her for many years to the Caribbean with his wife, Barbie. Between trips the boat was docked at Stine's Marina in Wingate. Ralph Ruark maintained her in ready condition for decades.

Even before *Barbara Batchelder*, Bronza was renowned for building recreational boats with inboard motors. He used mahogany for these

Lady Katie ready for painting. Wingate 1955.
Courtesy of Mary Parks Harding.

Launch of *Martha Lewis*. 26 October 1955.
Courtesy of Mary Parks Harding.

Painting *Rosie Parks* and *Martha Lewis*. October 1955.
Courtesy of Mary Parks Harding.

Rosie Parks on launch day. Wingate, October 1955.
Courtesy of Mary Parks Harding.

Bronza Parks in the boatyard. October 1955. After the launch of *Lady Katie*.
Courtesy of Mary Parks Harding.

and travelled to Baltimore to select his materials.

Three years after he built the 4 skipjacks, he was commissioned to build an 18' replica skipjack, intended for cruising. His customer was Willis Case Rowe, who wanted it built just like the earlier four boats. Rowe was 39 years old, a former prisoner of war, a lawyer and a writer for *U.S. News and World Report* magazine. Cody Parks, Osylee Lewis and Mary Parks Harding tell virtually the same story of what happened as work progressed on the small-scale skipjack.

Bronza and Rowe had established a price for the job, but then Rowe began asking for additions and alterations. They had agreed on galvanized nails, for example, but Rowe changed his mind in favor of brass screws for the entire project. This drove up the cost of building as well as the price, and Rowe and Bronza argued. Next, Rowe demanded narrower planking, on the grounds that his boat was smaller than the for-

Bronza Parks on newly launched *Barbara Batchelder.* 1956.
Courtesy of Mary Parks Harding.

mer skipkjacks. Mary Parks Harding remembers spending an hour on
the porch of Bronza's home talking to Rowe, after which she cautioned
her father about his customer, saying Rowe was unreliable. He had reportedly bought another boat and was short of funds.

Soon Rowe stopped making payments, and Bronza took out a lien
against the boat. Rowe argued that he was being overcharged, so he
and Bronza agreed to have an appraiser settle the issue. They agreed on
Jim Richardson, then the most knowledgeable and respected arbiter in
the area. Confident that the matter would be settled, Bronza drove his
Lincoln into town. At the time, the car was decorated with a pair of
donkeys, part of his campaign for County Commissioner as a Democrat.
He went to the office of the state's attorney and cancelled the lien.

Rowe drove to Jim Richardson's yard on LeCompte Bay, near Cambridge, to convince Richardson to drive with him to B. M. Parks Boatyard. Cody Parks was working for Jim at the time, and that day was up
the mast on the *Lady Alice,* "from South America." When Rowe drove up,
he found Jim and asked him to settle a dispute. Richardson was reluc-
tant to go with him, but did so when he learned that the circumstances
involved Bronza. "Rowe said that he was staying at Miss Parks' place in

Cambridge," according to Cody, "and that he was going down to Bronzie's to pay him off."

Rowe drove Richardson down to Wingate, where the three men met and Richardson sided with Bronza. Rowe agreed to pay what he owed and asked Jim to wait in the car. Richardson saw Rowe go back into the boathouse, he assumed to settle accounts. Shortly thereafter, Jim said he heard a sound like two wooden planks slapping together. When this was followed by two more slaps, he knew he was hearing gunfire. He ran to the building and found Bronza dead on the floor.

There had been another argument and Rowe said Bronza threatened him with a piece of wood. No one believed this then or later. Rowe had brought a revolver with him and shot Bronza twice in the head and once in the chest, killing him instantly. Two of the shots were apparently in the back of the head.

Malcolm Wheatley, a neighbor, came from next door to intercede, and Rowe tried to give him the gun. With Bronza face down on the floor, Wheatley told him to keep the gun until Dave Bradshaw, the sheriff, arrived. Jim Richardson went to Bronza's house near the shop to tell his wife what had happened. Osylee Lewis, arrived soon after the shooting and said that Rowe nearly paid for his actions on the spot. As a crowd began to gather, there was an impetus to hang Rowe from one of the beams in the boathouse that Bronza used to hoist engines. Osylee said, "Mac (Malcolm) and I sorta interfered, said, 'You better let the law take care of it. They'll be here soon.'" Dave Bradshaw arrived and took the gun from Rowe, placed him in handcuffs and drove him away.

And then it was over. More than a hundred townspeople gathered in and around the boathouse, struck with the awful truth that their employer, their friend, their family member, Bronza Parks, was dead at age 58.

Rowe was tried and entered an insanity plea. Over a series of trials and appeals, he was convicted of second-degree murder and, ultimately, spent six years in a state mental hospital. He had studied law and conducted his own appeal. After his release, he lived out the rest of his life in Cockeysville, Maryland, where he died in 2002.

The grief he left behind greatly affected the people of Wingate. Many were Bronza's relatives and all were related in some way to the main employer of the town. Bronza's wife, Katie, never recovered from the loss. According to their daughter, Mary, Katie rarely ventured from home the rest of her life, avoiding others' questions and sympathetic looks.

The unfinished boat sat for awhile at the yard, but ultimately a couple of young men sawed it into pieces.

Ralph Ruark ran the railway at Wingate after Bronza's death and maintained *Barbara Batchelder* for Mr. DuPont, with help from Cody Parks. Gail Sterling Joubert (GSJ) recalled that Ralph was her grandfather's "go-to" man at B.M. Parks. He helped Katie when Bronza died, and ran the boatyard for awhile. He died at his home in Toddville at age 78 in 2002.

Snooks Windsor became owner and operator of Powley's Marina at Wingate Harbor. When he sold it in 2014, he stayed on as manager.

Tom Dean, who also helped build *Martha Lewis*, passed away in 2001 at age 83.

Oneal Dean had a boat building business and a marine hardware store in Wingate. He was an active bluegrass and gospel musician until his death in 2006 at age 78.

When we spoke in 1993, Cody Parks was still the proud owner of *Dorothy Lee*, which Bronza built in 1933. He kept it in pristine condition at Stine's Marina in Wingate. Cody died in 2007 at age 77. *Dorothy Lee* survives under private ownership at Trappe, Md.

Several years before his death, Bronza Parks had seen the need for an ambulance as well as a fire truck for Wingate, and founded the Lakes and Straits Volunteer Fire Department. His family donated his boatyard and shop to the town and the fire station and meeting hall stand there now.

Calvert Parks
and *Dorothy Lee* at
Stine's Marina, Wingate,
September 1993.

Chapter 3
Jim Lewis and Osylee

The first owner of *Martha Lewis* was Jim Lewis, Jr. and his life's story was told to me by one who especially revered him, Osylee Lewis, his son.

Osylee proved to be a fountain of information about his father, about other watermen and about the skipjack *Martha Lewis*. We met a number of times and the tales he told were full of Bay lore and were rife with experiences, spoken in that wonderful accent still found along the Eastern Shore of the Chesapeake Bay.

We talked at length by phone and I later drove down to Wingate to meet him and his wife, Naomi. Both had gentle, kindly faces and seemed glad to meet me. At their comfortable home near the water, we sat and pored over old photos and scrapbooks and I recorded our conversation. Naomi served us a treat of crab cakes, while Osylee offered up a feast of local history.

Osylee was born in Wingate. He was one of the 10 children of James, Jr. and Floy Windsor Lewis, who were both from waterman families. Floy's father, Hudson Windsor, had owned two schooners and when Osylee was young he remembered him bringing watermelons to Wingate from Deal's (Deal) Island. Osylee's other grandfather, Jim Lewis, Sr. taught his son, Jim, Jr., the art of dredging, and "Jimmy" taught Osylee and his brothers.

Osylee's grandfather, James Matthew Lewis, Sr., had a skipjack named after his wife, Martha Miranda Dean Lewis. The skipjack was built in 1897 at Wingate and was 39' long. He called her *Martha M. Lewis*.

However, after years on the water, James Sr. grew weary. "One day in 1901," Osylee recalled, "my grandfather'd had it. He was sick of fishing and went middle of [the] deck and gave the boat over to my father. At

13 years old, he was captain of it. He took that boat over, an [my grandfather] went to work at Metal Tech!" Jim Sr. would catch the steam boat to Baltimore at the beginning of the week and return home by steam boat at the end of the week.

Osylee didn't remember much about his grandmother, Martha, except that she died young and that she was loved, so much so that when Jim Jr., "Jimmy" needed a skipjack, in 1954, he also named it after his mother, Martha Lewis. [see Appendix C, family tree]

Watermen harvest crabs in summer and oysters in winter. Osylee recalled that in the 1920s and 1930s, "crabs was awful scarce, so t' fill in, they used to haul watermelons by skipjack to Baltimore, Light Street. Go up Nanticoke River and get watermelons. That's before these trucks come up here and put us outta business." Historically, truck traffic came to the Eastern Shore in 1952 with the opening of the Chesapeake Bay Bridge.

James Matthew, Sr. and
Martha Miranda Dean Lewis.
c. 1905.
Courtesy of Osylee Lewis.

Osylee's family connections and his memory for details made him a perfect witness to skipjack pedigrees. The people and their boats were intricately connected. As he put it, "Everyone was related somehow. You'll find a lot of that in these water sections." Osylee elaborated:

> My brother-in-law, Ralph Ruark, owned *Wilma Lee*, which was Bronza's first skipjack. But it was first owned together by Uncle Asbury [Lewis] and Uncle Orville [Parks].
>
> Here's how come they had *Wilma Lee*. Asbury had

the *M.M. Travers* and Orville had the *Joy Parks*. They were coming down from Baltimore on the last day of the season and they stopped at Sharps Island buoy t' dredge some oysters. The ice had took [the buoy] away and Asbury got on a stony pile [ran aground]. There was one of these big buoy tenders anchored that could lift 'er right off the rock pile, but the captain couldn't get permission from Norfolk. He wouldn't do it. So *M.M. Travers* laid on that night and another day. That was rough, just ground 'er till it broke 'er in two. That's when 'e had the *Wilma Lee* built, him and Orville, by Bronza. That was around 1940.

Launch of *Wilma Lee* at Wingate. 1940.
Courtesy of Mary Parks Harding.

Stanley Norman was owned by Uncle Willis Windsor. My brother-in-law, Malcolm Wheatley, owned *Kathryn* and now Russel Dize has had her a long time. She was built down in Virginia, and has a copper ball on top. The *Ida May* used to be Orville [Parks]'s first dredge boat. He came outta service an' that was a gift from his father.

Osylee's father, Jim Lewis, Jr., oystered for many years with his bugeye *Clarence and Eva*, which had been built in 1889 in Cambridge. His nephew, Lemuel Lewis, remembered that the boat was unusually constructed. Its rounded hull was "double-planked, frame-built." Planking was fore-and-aft, inside and out. Rock salt was poured between the two layers, as preservative. Jim later "sold it to Deals Island," where it eventually sank. He also owned a Hoopers Island draketail, which he called *East Land*, and which had the unique feature of being able to back over thin ice and break the ice without injuring the boat.

Osylee's siblings were each tied in one way or another to skipjacks and the Bay.

> There were six boys and three girls, and one boy born dead. I'm the youngest of the boys that lived, and I had a sister that was younger than I was. My oldest sister, Edna, lives near the fire house. She's Malcolm Wheatley's wife. Malcolm owned [the skipjack] *Kathryn*.
>
> My oldest brother, David, had the *Krantz* [*H.M. Krentz*] built and Norris owned the *Elsworth*. They called it the 'Hellsworth.' Leon and Weller had the *Sterling* and *Stewart Brothers* buy boats. They would go out to the dredge boats and buy oysters from the watermen. Ya don't do any of that now. They bring 'em [oysters] right to the dock, but we used to stay out a week at a time, go up the Bay and put oysters in the hold.

Leon and Weller "Will" Lewis were in business together. They owned a bait and seafood company on Hoopers Island, and jointly owned the two buy boats. Leon also ran the buy boat *Agnes Elizabeth*, named for a daughter who died young. The two brothers also co-owned the skipjack *Mishap*. Leon's son, Leon, Jr. "Bud" was also a waterman. In October 1962 Bud was 20 years old and was crabbing on his boat *Rosa L.* with his 12-year old brother Lemuel, and a friend, 18-year-old Arvie Ruark, when the boat exploded, presumably from gasoline fumes in the hold. The fire was too intense for them to reach the life jackets. All were good swimmers, but two were badly burned. They floated briefly on empty gas cans, but could not hold on and drowned. Only Lemuel survived.

Will operated the buy boat *Sterling*, and carried crabs on deck from

Virginia with baitfish alewives in the hold. In about 1958 he sold all of his interest in the business to brother Leon. Osylee remembered that in his family, as in the whole community of Wingate, people looked after one another through good times and bad:

> It's one big family. We work together. When one's in need or in trouble, we help 'em out. You don't get that everywhere. I thank God I'm living in a place I'm proud of livin'. We may have a lot of mosquitoes home, but I can put up with that.

When Bronza Parks built three skipjacks in 1955, they stayed in the family. *Rosie Parks*, the fastest, belonged to Osylee's uncle (and Bronza's brother), Orville Parks. *Lady Katie* was first owned by Uncle Bronza, then by Eugene Wheatley. Eugene was the brother of Malcolm "Mac" Wheatley. Eugene owned *Lady Katie* with George Powley when they first began oystering. When Eugene died, George took over full ownership. *Martha Lewis* belonged to Osylee's father and brother. (For a listing of skipjacks and family trees, see Appendices B and C, respectively.)

We talked about the other dredge boats he remembered and it became clear that each boat had its own structural peculiarities and behavior. Builders and captains used trial-and-error, and borrowed ideas from each other to make practical modifications. This resulted in a fascinating diversity in performance, giving each boat a distinct personality. Skipjack design was never a constant, but rather an evolution.

> *Robert L. Webster* was one of the biggest and, for a dredge boat, most responsive on the Bay. It could be moderate weather when that captain twisted that wheel down on 'er and it'd go right around. The *Kathryn* and these boats [the three Bronza built together] would do the same thing. Did you know that a lot of these boats, the older makes especially, were real heavy to go around. That's why the newer skipjacks were so popular. They could work faster, so they could make more licks, what that means, drags. If you can get that dredge in an' go back, you can get several extry drags there in a day, so you'd make more money. Besides, the newer skipjacks didn't have to do all that caulkin' an'

all, like the older ones did. [In the older boats], the caulkin' cotton had a tendency to suck out over a period of time.

With shrinking harvests, productive oyster grounds became hard-fought territory and efficiency became more and more essential if a waterman were to scrape a living from the Bay. The Lewis family made one large and unsuccessful attempt at improving their oyster hauls, but, as Osylee recalled, it was boat design that proved their undoing.

At Fishin' Bay we had to move about. The boats we used were too large, so we had three skipjacks built down to Reedville, Virginia. My brothers took one, my father took one and I bought half the small boat with Pop. But all three were out of proportion and low to the water.

What happened, these boats were hard to manage. They would get to the windward, they have so much bigger sail, and they'd cut the wind off you in calm weather. And then you got a job! And they were built so low that your deck was all awash, especially if you caught any amount of oyster. You were just in between. They weren't appropriate. We called one *Mistake*, which was Norris's boat, and the other 'un we called *Mishap*. Weller and Leon had her. Mine and Pop's was *Sister*, sister to the other two. She must have been 51', from the stern to the bowsplit.

Lot o' times, I was the one out on the bowsplit to reef the jib. Kinda funny, this rocket of water comes up, an' ya' have to watch yourself.

Most captains had a few friends or relatives who worked with them on the water, but generally they relied on African-American crews ("colored crews" in the parlance of the day), especially on dredge boats. The men came from as far away as Nanticoke, across Fishing Bay, and from Cambridge, though a few lived on Liner's and Blackwater Roads west of Crapo. The work was grueling and the pay marginal, but when times were lean, there were always crews available. The usual pay on dredge boats was: one-half of the profits for the boat and captain, and one-half divided among the crew. Food, fuel, repairs, and equipment costs were taken out of the boat/captain's portion. Wingate dredge boat owners were known for treating their crews respectfully. Slackers are not tolerated by fellow crewmen, but hard workers stayed with their captains for years and even generations.

Osylee's experience, however, gives us another take on crew life when he was one of its members:

> We'd get crew from Nanticoke. They'd come aboard Monday morning; they'd be half drunk. It'd be 'fore Wednesday before they'd straighten up. Meantime, I'd still have to go aboard. 'Least I'd know what I's a doin'.
>
> I was the one Pa actually depended on to keep the winders goin' and the dredges, and the yawl boat motor and to keep check on the colored crew. And o' course he was schoolin' me on ketchin' marks for an oyster bar. We found, after 30 years, sometimes they got depleted. But then, just about the time you've forgotten about it, they spring up again.
>
> Every boat has a different peculiarity. Some are low at the bow and ya can't steer as well, when y're a work boat. Did you know the *Martha Lewis* has a ton or two of stone aft for ballast? You know why? Well, she draws back, when she's under sail, a little bit.
>
> The captain has to know his boat almost like hisself. If that boat is not headin' into the wind like it should, they move that mast a little forward. But you've gotta be careful, get it just right. It'll come up too much and you won't be havin' the speed. The captain knows that you keep puttin' more stone in there till that boat comes up. They call it trimmin'. When ya lower the yawl boat, that sets the bow down, too.
>
> Also, it's a known fact that the more wood ya have under water, the more control you have in rough weather. These are a rough weather boat.

Osylee clearly took pride in the knowledge of the Bay and its boats that he learned at his father's side. His father's skills were legendary.

Floy Windsor and
James Matthew Lewis, Jr. 1950s.
Courtesy of Osylee Lewis.

James Matthew Lewis, Jr. c. 1962.
Courtesy of Osylee Lewis.

Pop has a reputation. He could catch some oysters. If you ever talk to any watermen, they know Captain Jimmy Lewis. Pop could be lying down in 'is bunk and, anywhere from here up the Bay, he could tell you where he was. If you gave him depth of water, and what kinda bottom it was, muddy bottom or broken bottom, he'd say, 'well, we ought to be off Barren Islan' Light'! I could find my way around pretty good an all, but he was ... I don't know ... it seems like there's some people just talented for that, and he was one of 'em. He started early enough, but that don't always work, either. There's some people does carpentry work all their life, but they fail to be a master craftsman.

Pop had a little book an', when oysters got scarce, every night he would look in that little book. Say, 'the wind's northeast tamarra, we ought ta be layin' up'n that age.' (He called it 'age' steada 'edge.') In other words, if this rock was runnin' this way, you'd prefer the wind to be so's you could carry the sail. Otherwise, where the oysters were slim, you'd cut across the rock and only get part of it. Now with Pa dredgin', you could work around there so fast.

A fella from Cambridge calls drudgers from here boat-hook drudgers. Ya take that boat hook an' feel that line, an' the way it jumps, you could tell whether you was catchin' oysters or shell. It isn't everybody could do that, but Papa was the best one. He'd have a boat hook across 'ere, and he always had buoys handy there. He'd tell one of us boys, 'get ready,' and then we'd throw the buoys. You'd find what they'd call lumps away from the main bars. He was good at it. Sometimes I'd seen him lose half a day an' only have a bushel or two. But end o' day come, he'd have his limit.

I want to add this. The timing is very important, when to take the sails off, especially when it's blowin' heavy or if ya use the yawl boat. The timing is very important. Father and son knew what to expect of each other, especially in rough weather.

[Pop] was easy goin' an' was really religious. He was superintendent of [Wingate Methodist Church] for 46 years. He was a very caring person. I don't think I ever saw him mad in my life. An' if he was ever feelin bad, an' if he ever went an' laid down, you'd say he was really sick.

Pop had an amazin' Boston terrier. He would tell him anywhere from one to five times to turn around. He could distinguish that. You could start from five, 'now turn around five times.' He would do it an' Pop would give him a piece of hot dog. There was nobody [else] home after Mom died, so that dog and him was brothers. After father died, that dog died. It only lived a few months.

Lt. Earl Jerome Lewis. c. 1959.
Courtesy of Osylee Lewis.

In 1954, Jim Lewis went in with another of his sons, Earl, to buy and operate a new dredge boat, which he called *Martha Lewis*, after his mother. Earl was 37 years old at the time and had joined the state police force in 1942. He was a well respected law enforcement officer who received commendations for heroism in three rescues on the Bay. Concerned that it could have been seen as a conflict of interest for a state trooper to own a dredge boat, they left Earl's name off the boat title.

Osylee spoke fondly of his brother, "He was the youngest lieutenant in the State of Maryland and was up for captain. He was an expert swimmer and loved to fish."

On April 1, 1962, Osylee had loaned him a boat to go fishing near Ordinary Point on the Sassafras River and, somehow, Earl Lewis went missing. The boat was found drifting the next day, with fish in it. An extensive search included divers and a section of the Sassafras was dragged. The search covered a large area of the river between Cecil and Kent Counties.

Two weeks after he disappeared, Earl's body was found in the river a mile from where he had been tending his fish nets. The medical examiner pronounced drowning the cause. He was 44 years old and left behind his wife, Katherine (Kitty), two daughters and a son. Jim Lewis stopped oystering after that and sold the boat. He lived two more years.

Osylee served in the Pacific Theater during the Second War in the Army Corps of Engineers. He married Arie Naomi Parks during the war and the couple had two children, Jim and Anna. Osylee said:

> I oystered up until my father got disabled. I graduated [from Crapo High] in 1940 and went aboard a dredge boat. The first one I was on was a bugeye, the *Clarence and Eva*. Then Uncle Sam got me from '43 to '45.

Oystering is how I guess I got to be a cox'n on a landing craft in World War II. They had five special brigades an' I was in the fourth, an' they wanted us guys that had been on the water. Actually, I guess we was one of the best trained outfits they was. We already had our boats an' everything loaded on APA ships to invade Japan, the time the bomb was dropped. Otherwise I might not 'a' been here.

When I was discharged, I came back, started on a dredge boat up until the late 1950's.

While Osylee worked on the water and he and Naomi also manufactured crab pots. Naomi was also a crab picker at one of the several local crab houses and continued in this enterprise for most of the rest of her life.

The seafood economy has struggled, and today only one crab house remains, the Dorchester Crab Company, on the east side of Wingate harbor. On the west side of the harbor is the new Honga River Oyster

Osylee and Dan Lewis.
September 1994.

Company, another answer to the changing times. Here, in response to dwindling natural populations, oysters are propagated in wire cages, where more dependable harvests can be controlled.

In about 1958 Osylee needed steadier income and went to work as a repairman for the Sears, Roebuck Company based in Cambridge. He said, "In the service, I was an electrician part of the time, an' I went to school for radio and TV work after I left the water." He helped his father at home and on the water on weekends. But as Jim, Jr. gradually slipped into Parkinsonism, his days on the water became numbered. Osylee's

Dan Lewis and grandfather Osylee Lewis
racing *Martha Lewis*. October 1995.

Dan Lewis carrying on waterman's tradition on
his great-grandfather's skipjack. October 1995.

Lewis family at Havre de Grace reception, 23 January 1994.
Left to right: Osylee and Naomi Lewis, the author, Anna and Jim Lewis.
Courtesy Elizabeth Rawl

nephew, Lemuel Lewis, said that Jim knew it was time to go ashore and told him the story of when he became certain. One early morning in the winter of 1961, Jimmy went down to the dock and went aboard his dredge boat *Martha Lewis*. He waited, but there was no crew. He figured it was their way of telling him that he needed to stop. His family cared for him until his death in 1964.

Osylee used his Bronza-built workboat, *Anna Arlene*, until he retired from Sears. He also devoted his time to the Wingate Methodist Church, where he was a lay speaker. He was a member of the volunteer fire department, was a Boy Scout leader and was an active member of the local American Legion Post.

After *Martha Lewis* was restored, Osylee and his grandson, Dan Lewis, sailed with Allen Rawl and me on the *Martha Lewis* in several skipjack races. Osylee tended the main sheet and advised the captain, while Dan managed the jib.

Osylee Lewis passed away in 2012 and Naomi followed him in 2015.

Chapter 4

Dave Faulkner

In 1962 Jim Lewis sold *Martha Lewis* to another waterman, Dave Faulkner, who moved her to Tilghman Island. I met Dave at a roadside diner in the autumn of 1993, and he told me his story.

Years ago there were lots of boats...schooners, bugeyes and many skipjack on the Bay. I've seen 50, 60 or 70 boats workin' around Sharp's Island, back in the 1940s and '50s. My family has been fishing since they came to this country. I've even traced back to where our family came over on a ship named the *Agroom* in 1665 from Scotland. They landed in Oxford (Maryland) and the captain's name was Capt. Groom. I've got the papers, the manifests.

My family has owned boats for years. My Uncle Joe, Josiah Faulkner, built a lot of them. He lived at Fairbank and owned a lot of schooners, bugeyes, and skipjacks. He owned *Virginia Bell*, *Queen*, one named *Pluck*, and *Lily of the Valley*. My cousin, Jimmy Faulkner, owned *F. C. Lewis*.

When I was 16, I started dredging, in 1945, with an old fellow on Tilghman's Island named Cap'n Buck Murphy on a boat named the *Wilma Florence*. Then I went with Darryl Larrimore's grandfather, Capt. Glendy [pronounced Glendai] Larrimore. He had the *Laura Barkley*. After that I went to the service in the Korean War. When I got out in 1953 I bought a boat, the *Ethel Lewis*, built in 1898. She had a Model A Ford [engine] in the middle of the deck, and a 6-cylinder

Studebaker in the yawl boat. There wasn't any hand winders left around then, though they were used up until the early '30s.

Dave completely rebuilt *Ethel Lewis* except for some of her bottom. He worked her and eventually sold her to a man on Sheepshead Bay, Long Island, New York, who used her for a pleasure boat. That's when he bought *Martha Lewis*.

We leafed through a scrapbook he brought with him and stopped at a picture of a respectable gentleman.

Here's a picture of my third cousin, Capt. Tom Faulkner. He used to live down lower part a' Tilghman's Islan'. At 92, he was the head of the treasury at Talbot County. Years and years ago he had a grocery store, lower part a' the island. That's where the boats used to anchor, out in Black Walnut Harbor, and come ashore and a' course they'd buy their food or rope, cotton bagging for their dredges, all that. He carried ever'thing, like a hardware store, grocery store combined. That's where we fitted up.

Faulkner's time as owner of *Martha Lewis* offers a window into the business of being a waterman.

I paid Capt. Jim Lewis $6,000 for *Martha Lewis*. She was in good shape then, and I only had to put a few pieces of wood into her. I did my own work back then. We hauled her up every year, painted her sides and bottom, at Fluhardy's boatyard on Tilghman. And I used to leave her the last years over t' Capt'n Jim Richardson's place, below Cambridge, Le Count's [LeCompte] Bay. I'd anchor 'er out there, and he took care of 'er for me. He lived right there, and he hauled her up in the fall. When I bought 'er, Cap'n Jim [Lewis] had the yawl boat at his home, sittin' back in the marsh. We pushed 'er over, and I ran 'er around to Kirwan's Boat Yard [Wingate].

I think the deck engine was a Model A, but I put in a 4-cylinder Ford Industrial Engine for the winders.

Cap'n Adam Capsack at Tilghman made the dredges. He worked for Glen L. Martin, all during the War. He was a man who didn't have much schoolin', but he was a good blacksmith. He could take a piece a' steel and make anything.

Like many skipjack owners, Faulkner experimented with the sail plan to improve *Martha Lewis'* performance.

When I bought her, she had a 42' boom and I just didn't think it was long enough, so I put a 53' boom on 'er. As far as I was concerned, the more mainsail ya had, the more you could luff up into the wind when you were pullin' yer dredges in really light air. That mainsail just kep' 'er choppin' up. Of course that size was for workin'. For racing it wouldn'ta made any difference. The mast I remember was 72'.

Another innovation Dave used was a long spar called a "club", designed to increase the sail height above the top of the mast. Laced to the luff of the sail's head, it's center could be hauled to the masthead, to increase the sail height 3' or 4'.

Sail makers were kept busy in those days. Faulkner described what it took to maintain a skipjack, beginning with buying sails from Downs Curtis, of Oxford, who was in the business with his brother:

These were two black fellas who were in the business for a long time, and were good sail makers. O' course, back when I was dredgin' we used canvas sails. So they made us a lot a' suits a' sails. A suit wouldn't last us more than 5 years, so they made at least 3 or 4 suits for me.

Anyway, I had t' put a mast in 'er. The old mast that Bronzie put in had rotten wood in it, right at the partners, in fact, two or three places. Capt. Jim Richardson went with me over near Reliance, right near t' Delaware line, and this was the first that I'd ever seen this little deal: He cut a little tree about the height of his eyes, about an inch and a half in diameter. He saw the tree he liked, (he wanted 90'), and walked off from the base of it 90'. He laid down and he got me to hold the piece of wood that he'd cut, at his feet. He sighted over it and that's the way he got his 90'. The tree was 3' at the stump. He 4-squared it, 8-squared it, 16-squared it, planed it, and we had just about all heart. It was a good mast. That's the one my cousin, Ellis Berridge, blew out. We made the mast of green wood in October and started dredging in November. I heard Capt. Dize replaced my mast with a piece of fir from Oregon.

I financed the purchase of *Martha Lewis* through the bank. Back then a third of the profits went to the boat and gasoline was taken out of this. The other two-thirds was divided among the 7 of us, after groceries were taken out. Oysters were sold cheap. Three dollars a bushel was good. Lot a' times they were half of that.

We oystered if the winds were less than 40 knots, and played poker when it was calm. Even a faint breeze could be used for dredging.

We talked about work on the water, and about the rigors of sailing on the Bay in the winter.

Quite a few men were lost during the time I worked on the Bay. They'd lose a man overboard every now and then. Twice, I lost a man overboard and was lucky enough to get 'em both times. One day it was blowin' a gale northeast, snowing, cold. Back in those days we wore sheep-lined coats, leather, and this man was reefin' the jib. When he threw the jib away off the Samson post, he got on the leeward side and the jib sheet pulled 'im over. One of our men reached his hand over the side and was lucky enough to catch him as he went by. The fella held on and we pulled him aboard. Another time I lost a man overboard, yawl boatin'. We were pushin' in, and just turned around and got him. But there were others that were not lucky and ended up drowned. Junior Willing lost a man one day when we were dredging on Stone Rock. I think it was a relative. It wasn't too long after that he quit dredgin'. It's kinda bad, goin' home to tell the wife and kids about it, ya know. Junior has a railroad down t' Deal Island now.

In 1962 I bought *Martha Lewis* from James Lewis, and, in 1964, I started a corporation and transferred her from myself to Martha Lewis, Inc. I later changed it to Faulkner Enterprises, Inc. I dissolved Martha Lewis, Inc. and, in 1992, dissolved Faulkner Enterprises. I used her only for oystering, and I captained her until the last coupla months. I was in the canning business and my brother-in-law, Lee Swann, captained her for awhile. When I was sailin' he was one of my crew. Other members were Richard Radcliff, Andrew and Lee Finney, and they were with me the whole time I dredged.

Dave sailed *Martha Lewis* in some of the skipjack races held before the oystering season. He raced *Martha Lewis* at the Deal Island Labor Day Races, and said:

Dave Faulkner at the helm of *Brenda Jean*. Wicomico River. October 1993.

I also raced her a few times after I sold her to Dan Dize. His son-in-law, Gene Tyler, called me and asked me to race it.

Here's an article about me, uses my full name, George Davis Faulkner. It talks about the Deal Island races when we would stop crabbin' and tune up the skipjacks for the race. We'd get up early, tend the crab traps before sunrise, go in for breakfast and then set out for the race. I sailed the *Martha Lewis* with all her dredging gear aboard and with barnacles on the bottom. My son, wife and 6 or 8 friends and I would sail her the 60 miles from Tilghman Island to Deal Island.

In 1967 after 2 decades on the water and 5 years with *Martha Lewis*, Dave Faulkner quit dredging and sold his boat to Dan Dize. The day we spoke he had come down from his home in Federalsburg, Maryland, where he was in the canning and trucking business. He drove me out to the Wicomico Yacht Club, where he kept his large and comfortable cabin cruiser, *Brenda Jean*. As we motored along the Wicomico River, we passed the moldering bones of the once proud bugeye *Mamie Mister*, sinking in the mud at Whitehaven.

Dave died at age 83 in Seaford, Delaware in 2013.

Chapter 5
Dan Dize and the Tylers

Capt. Daniel Austin Dize was born on 19 August 1908 at Ewell on Smith Island, and became a seasoned waterman and ship owner. He married his first wife, Thelma Louise Kitchens, in 1930 and moved in the 1950s to Tilghman Island, where he bought and worked a total of 5 skipjacks and 2 cargo freighters. He retired in 1980 and in 1989 moved back to Smith Island with his second wife, Madeline Bradshaw.

Smith Island is home to several hundred persons, each with historical ties to the water. The cluster of islands hosts three small towns, with modest homes, and several churches. On October 1993 I travelled to Smith Island to meet Dan and his wife. I left at noon from the dock at Crisfield on *Captain Jason*, a mail and supply boat. We entered Ewell harbor and tied up at the dock. I hopped off and was directed to Rhodes Point along an old macadam road. Along the road were a number of fishermen's houses, and I found Dan and Madeline Dize's comfortable two-story home near the water. They were expecting me, and Madeline had made a feast of mashed potatoes, crab cakes, beef and corn. We talked as we ate and for a long time afterward. I asked if I could record the conversation, and they seemed glad to have their history appreciated.

Dan was 85 years old and had a weathered face and hands. By dint of a lifetime dedicated to skipjacks and oystering, he was brimming with a wealth of experience in his craft. He had been a shrewd and relatively successful businessman. Before *Martha Lewis*, he owned the skipjack *Fannie L. Daugherty* which he bought in about 1932 and dredged for 35 years. During this time he also owned *Annie Lee*, another skipjack, which he said was later sunk in the Virgin Islands when she tore out her centerboard well. While he owned *Martha Lewis*, he also ran two grain freighters, *Marylander* and *Henrietta Frances*. He worked *Martha* for 6 years, but owned part or all of her for 18 years. He ceded half-ownership to Etheldeen (Deenie), his daughter, and her husband, Gene A. Tyler, in 1973. Deenie and Gene owned her outright in 1986.

Dan came from a large Smith Island family. His father and grandfather were boat captains. His parents were Theodore Dize (1867-1922) and Maggie Venora Tyler Dize (1869-1934) and they had thirteen children. Two died at birth, leaving 5 boys and six girls. Dan was the youngest.

As a youngster Dan remembered working on the skipjack *Claude W. Somers*. He worked for his cousin and earned $12 a week, working both dredges, and "cullin' off both sides." He remembered that the leeward dredge would usually come up on its back. He'd have to flip it over, cull the oysters, throw back the dredge and jump to the windward dredge to haul it in, dump it, throw it overboard and cull the oysters on that side, then repeat the process over and over again, "and I was getting' $12 a week!"

Dan was 14 years old when his father died, but even before that, he was a waterman:

> I was unfortunate in the education line. I was taken out of school when I was nine years old and had finished three weeks of the fourth grade. Money was tight, but Daddy could always get a job. He'd sell oysters to the packin' houses t' Crisfield. He'd go over the Potomac and other places. He had a two-masted bugeye, the *James T. Blaine*, and when he died they sold her away to North Carolina. Daddy was offered a thousand dollars for 'er just before he died, on his death bed. He said, 'she ain't fer sale'. My mother got 450 dollars for 'er.

> One time Daddy went to Cedar Point, just below the Potomac River bridge; that's where he would anchor. The oysters there were fresh but fat. So, this time, on his way over from Crisfield, he had a head wind all night long. No one had any sleep, but Daddy went below to get some rest. He had a 38 nickel-plated revolver. You've seen how they break open, and they've got a ketch when you slam 'em to. Well, this ketch was

broke, and he had a strong rubber band from the ketch to back around the trigger guard. They were sailin' up the Potomac River when he went below and fell asleep. This n---- crewman got the gun out from under his pillow, and the only thing that saved him was he musta thought the band hindered the firing and took it off. When he pulled the trigger the plunger just smitted the cap and it didn't go off. He snapped it at Daddy and my brother and it didn't go off.

Then he laid the revolver on the table and unlatched the cupboard where we kept tools. He took an old hatchet out'n there. Because the bumps (bunks) aboard the boat were so close to the ceiling, he had to use the hatchet flatways. Every time he hit my daddy, it would cut 'im up and bruise 'im. He hit my daddy 13 times and hit my brother 8. Daddy didn't do well after that. He couldn't build his blood back up. Then he went into TB and died two years later. Anyway, that's howcome I didn't have no education. At the end I'd go aboard to help him. My brother Rodney [born 1905] and I could haul the anchor. My sister went along, too. She was big, healthy and strong. My mother'd go aboard part time to cook.

Dan remembered well his early days on the water.

We always had a push boat. I could run it when I was 8, a Five Hubbard Vic'try, they called it, a single cylinder. It ran with no spark plug; it wasn't made with one. It had a flat piece on the front of 'er and what is called an igniter. A bolt came out here, and another, there. It had a timer, and a rod with a spring, and an eccentric went around her crankshaft to trip a spring up and down. If we'd want to go back on 'er, we'd put a finger on that spring and stop it from crimpin' an' she'd cut off and, just as she made the last kick, you'd let go and she'd go backward.

We always had winders in my day, but I had to

dredge orsters with my brother-in-law with cranks. We'd hand crank the dredges. I heard my daddy say that on his pungy boat, they're dredgin' in these stones on Silas Middle or on Nor'west Middle, and the crank handle kicked back on 'em and threw 'em clean up in the fores'l. My daddy used to dredge with his pungy and also freighted orsters, lumber and wood. If he didn't have no lumber or freight, he didn't go out.

The work of dredging required simultaneously tending the jib and mainsail. Particularly in heavy, cold weather, tending a sail could be dangerous work. Since the jib is tacked to the end of the bowsprit ("bowsplit," in Bay parlance), its lowering and reefing require working out over the bow wave, often in choppy conditions. Dan described the challenge of working from the bowsprit:

I was a bowsplit man from the time I ever started a'goin' on boats. The bowsplit can get as slipp'ry as a greezed eel. You go out there when it's a-sleetin' or snowin' or rainin' or whatever, wi' her bow snuttin' down, you can imagine what! So when I got my own boat, I put a strip a' wood on either side of 'er [the bowsprit] so you wouldn't slide off. An' I put a slant on it on either side. It would be level when she listed, ya get me? I made 'em outta redwood and varnished 'em. Man, that was beautiful! I did that on *Maggie Lee*.

Beneath the bowsprit a boathand stood on footropes while tending the jib. Dan remembered:

Me an' another fella was reefin' a jib one time the hemp foot rope broke, an' I went down in the water so deep, I had ta catch the bowsplit, but I landed my foot on the bobchain or jib chain, I don't know which, an' tuck water in the hip pocket.

An' he caught on too, this other fella, he was from Tangier. We both caught, and we weren't hurt by it. But if we had went underneath the boat, she'd a' beat us ta' death 'fore we got to the other end of 'er. It was rougher'n I don't know what. When I got a boat, the first improvement I done to 'er was put double chain footropes.

Dan said he bought *Martha Lewis* in 1967 against the advice of his wife and friends. He bought her from Dave Faulkner for $7,000 on a Saturday night, and dredged and spatted on Monday morning and for 7 weeks thereafter. The State of Maryland for many years paid watermen to dredge juvenile oysters (spat) from its planting beds. Watermen were paid by the bushel to dredge, haul and reseed on state oyster preserves. Early in his career he was paid 5 cents a bushel and remembered being paid $17.50 for carrying 350 bushels, using a crew of 5, plus the captain. "I remember time they planted [spat] back a' Poplar Islan'. They used to let it stay 2-3 years before they'd open it up. An' they opened it up an' I think it was 4 hunerd and 14 bushels I caught that day."

He recalled that while he was in Baltimore at the hospital bedside of his first wife, Thelma:

> I let *Martha Lewis* out to Ellis Berridge [who happened to be Dave Faulkner's cousin]. He was dredgin' 'er and carried 'er mast off. Oh, by the way, I put a mast in the *Annie Lee*, cost $100 all set and ready t' go. I put a mast in the *Darity* [*Fannie L. Daugherty*], I think it was $200 or somethin'. When Ellis broke that mast off, I carried her to Jim Richardson's yard to that place t' L'Counts [LeCompte] Bay, just below Cambridge. And how much did it cost?! You ain't gonna believe it, 1400 and some dollars. I swear ya can't believe a such. That's the mast that's in 'er now. The boom came from the *Robert C. Webster*, but not the mast. I scarfed the end of the boom. The mast was a squarr piece o' timber, cause I was there when Jim cut it. I think the timber come from Baltimore in the squarr. I think 'er mast was 68' long. O.K., it was a 72' piece a' timber, and I was always sorrah that I cut it off, especially after I heard what Orville Parks said: 'don't worry about havin' a wide sail, have a tall one.'

Dan often took *Martha Lewis* to Richardson's yard when he needed major work done on her. Once she started taking on water and he assumed she needed caulking. Calvert Parks was working there at the time and told him, "somethin's definitely wrong 'cause Uncle Bronzie ain't have carkin'." Bronza Parks built his skipjacks without seams between the bottom or side planks. Calvert told Dan, "the nails are ate up in it." They pulled her out on the railway and the bottom looked perfect, but when they tapped on it, several planks fell out. Electrolysis had eaten away the formerly sturdy ship nails. All had to be replaced.

As we talked, Dan easily took us back to his days on the water, as if he were in the moment.

When you're dredgin' and you reef, you've got to slack yer sail down to outhaul 'er and pull 'er tight on the end of the boom, and when you've got your reef points tied, then you heist it back up. Nine times out of 10, the first reef you can do, and [the club] won't come down below yer jacks [lazyjacks]. But if you put the second or third reef in, the top of yer club will come down below the jacks. Then, when you go t' heist it up and the wind is into it, it blows yer sails underneath your jacks and you can't heist it up. You have to get a headway on 'er and bring 'er up into the wind for the club to come up under your jacks. Or, if your downhaul is on that side, you might get a couple a' men t' hike it up and get it in that way.

There's differ'nt kinds of mud in this Bay that will really hold you like a big anchor when the drudge hits it. That 'Chinese mud, they call it, t' Solomon's Island, Pertuxent [Patuxent] is one. Then there's the inky and soft mud that's all over the Bay, even above the Bay Bridge. When it gets your drudge full, it's really heavy. The other comes from where they've drudged the channels out, here and there. Sometimes you'd get that stuff in your drudge and couldn't wash it out. That's clay.

One time [the captain] on the *Ruby Ford* said I was acatchin', alandin' a lot a little ones, but I didn't know it at the time the inspectors come aboard me; there's three of um. All three of um went to a differ'nt pile.

They scrambled through a lot of um, and then stood up an' looked at one another. And I didn't know what was agoin' on. One said to the other, 'I don't see nuthin' wrong with 'um. I thought they were just makin' remarks, an' they let me go. Come to find out [that captain] reported me ketchin' small 'ns. Get me? Lot a that goes on in life ya know.

The design of a skipjack determined most of its performance, but Dan and son-in-law Gene were innovators when it came to getting the most power and speed out of theirs. Though Dan and then Gene worked the *Fannie L. Daugherty* for 30 years, she could never outhaul *Martha Lewis*, especially in light air. Dan was very strong in his opinion that the mast be 70' long, especially after he regretfully shortened the mast on *Martha Lewis*. He said that the height of the mainsail mattered more than the surface area. When he used the club to increase height, the boom would come up, but he said this didn't matter.

The *Darity* never had as much pullin' power in 'er sails as the *Martha Lewis*. With the drudges I had, I'd throw um overboard, and I'd be solid anchored in the mud, until I'd wind um up. When you'd get um up you'd go again. You'd take up some line, two or three turns on the spool. If you took up too much and yer goin' too fast, you ain't got nuthin' on yer drudge. Well the *Martha Lewis*, I'd throw her dern drudge on that mud, an' generally it was just the same as I was on hard bottom. And she'd get 'm too.

Like most skipjack captains, Dan was drawn to the autumn workboat races, as much for the adventure as for the trophy money he could earn. He and his son-in-law, Gene Tyler, won more than 20 racing trophies. They ascribed some of their success to the mainsail club. At some point, a 2' strip of canvas was removed from the foot of Martha's mainsail. He didn't say who did it or why, only that *Martha Lewis* stopped winning races thereafter.

Dan gradually ceded ownership of *Martha Lewis* to his daughter and son-in law, Deenie and Gene Tyler. When Gene died of a brain tumor in 1991, Deenie and her two sons, Troy and Gilbert, sold her to Willie

Capt. Dan Dize, Captain Gene Tyler, and Etheldeen Tyler with with winner's cup. Chesapeake Appreciation Days Skipjack Race. c. 1974.

Roe. Dan had a particular love for the boat and regretted its loss. "She weren't supposed to sell that boat to nobody but me. And I would have bought her from Willie Roe. I knew she was for sale. But I can't see nuthin' and I'm old. After my heart operation the doctor told me I can't lift over 5 pounds. When you get in this water business and you can't do that, you ain't gonna do very good."

Dan had two daughters and two sons. Etheldeen (Deenie) was born in 1933 and her sister, Elestine, in 1938. Gilbert Austin "Gibby" Dize was born in 1931 and was a waterman. Herman Russell Dize was born in 1941 and began his work on the water as a teenager. Russell owned the Tidewater Clam Company, then A.D.S. Seafood, both on Tilghman Island. For years he was the respected owner and captain of the skipjack

Deenie Tyler at home at her parent's former house, on Tilghman Island. September 1993. Wind vane was carved by Dan Dize.

Kathryn, and now takes out crabbing charters.

After my trip out to Smith Island, I visited Deenie and son Troy at
the Tyler family home on Tilghman Island. The Tyler house was large
and comfortable, with a skipjack wind vane in the front yard that Dan
Dize had carved years ago. The large family room was a museum dedicated to *Martha Lewis*, complete with a wooden model of her and shelves
covered with trophies she had won over the years. We pored over scrapbook pictures of family and friends, many taken at the races. A long-
time friend, Henry Reeser, appeared in many of them. Henry owned a
marina, was a blacksmith and repaired Gene's dredges, but mainly he
was a good friend. Deenie said her father was an avid racer, until his
eyes began to fail him in later years.

Gene Tyler had worked *Martha Lewis* out of Tilghman Island for 18
years. He was no longer around to tell his own stories, but his spir-
it was certainly still there among his trophies and his family. Deenie
said that he was a lifetime waterman. He dredged in the winter and
fished for crabs and rockfish in the summer. Troy said that when he
worked for awhile with his father, on *Martha Lewis*, he usually tended
the starboard dredge. He told me that Gene had the same crew for years.

"They would work here [Tilghman] before Christmas, and then, when it started to get colder, they would move down to Solomon's Island, where it didn't freeze up so quickly. The crewmen were Eddie Somers, Lee Tyler, Homer Tyler and Larry Marsh. Bobby Lee Tyler crewed for at least 10 years before he moved to Smith Island. He treated them all like one family."

Dan Dize passed away in 2003 at McCready Hospital in Crisfield, Maryland, at age 95.

Martha's next owner, Willie Roe, had her for two years before he found that the cost of upkeep was unsustainable. When Allen

**Captain Gene Tyler.
Courtesy of Etheldeen Tyler.**

Rawl and I went to pick her up from him at Tilghman, he took us out on his fishing boat, after rockfish. Willie was gracious and we came home with plenty of fish, but no new stories about *Martha Lewis*. Willie's fishing boat eventually succumbed to age, and he had a new 42-footer built, the *Big Will*. In 2016, at age 82, Capt. Willie runs fishing charters out of Tilghman Island, Maryland.

Capt. William Roe on *Martha Lewis*. Tilghman Island. September 1993.

~ Chapter 6 ~

Builder's Log

Shipbuilder Allen Rawl kept a detailed log, chronicling the restoration of **Martha Lewis.** *The text of that log follows, edited to minimize repetition yet retain the essential information about the project. This documentation will be particularly instructive to those interested in skipjack construction details. Its abbreviation regretfully leaves unlisted the names and important contributions of dozens of crew members, museum and boat school volunteers, of donors and city and county officials who made the effort possible. Coast Guard inspections and clearances were a regular occurrence. Allen notes his appreciation for guidance offered by Gerry Trobridge, master shipsmith, Capt. Stanley Larrimore, owner of sister-ship* **Lady Katie,** *and Fred Hecklinger, Chesapeake Bay Marine Surveyor, among others. Many of the terms and boat parts he refers to can be confusing at first, but are more clearly defined in the glossary that follows the log.*

Allen Rawl

This builder's log begins in the fall of 1993 with the purchase of the skipjack *Martha Lewis* from her owner by Randolph George and her arrival at Havre de Grace for restoration. The work will take place at the Concord Point Lighthouse Park at a temporary yard provided by the Havre de Grace Maritime Museum and the City.

Between 27 September and 15 October, 1993, arrangements were made for facilities, fencing, construction trailer, power, permits and timber.

OCTOBER 16. With the assistance of a crew from Aberdeen Proving Ground, we began dismantling all equipment, sails, rigging and spars from her hull. Each piece was tagged and inventoried and secured at the yard and at the Chesapeake Bay Wooden Boat School.

OCTOBER 22 - 23. Our lead shipwright, Sam Jones, arrived from South Bristol, Maine, and we began building the cribbing to support *Martha's* hull. At the town dock, two large cranes lifted her out of the water. They placed her on a flatbed trailer, which moved her through town to the yard, where she was securely blocked.

First signs of decay. September 1993. Courtesy Allen Rawl.

OCTOBER 27 - 30. Sunny and beautiful, turning to rain and cold. We began dismantling *Martha* and the obviously rotten decking and deck beams were the first to go. The enthusiastic crew is advised to preserve any parts that are suitable for replacement or preservation in the Museum archives. The boat was stripped of her trail boards, exposing rot in the stem, a bit of bad news. Earlier inspection of the stem gave no indication of rot there. We removed part of her covering boards, her chain plates, hatch coamings and bobstay irons. Rot was uncovered along the top of several deck beams.

Rotten stem. September 1993. Courtesy of Allen Rawl.

NOVEMBER 3 - 5. The rotted stem was removed and set aside in two pieces. Apparently the upper half had been replaced years ago and the new upper piece was simply butted to the lower remaining half – not a practice I would favor. We think that we have now discovered all rot that can be found.

NOVEMBER 6 - 11. Lovely fall weather. We took the lines off *Martha*, using a measuring device I designed and that the crew built over the past several days. These were recorded numerically in just 2 hours and

LEFT:
Stem removed.
Demonstrating keel, keel shoe,
staves, knightsheads, side
planks, Samson post.

BOTTOM:
Taking lines for offset
drawings. September 1993.
Images courtesy of Allen Rawl.

New stem October 1993. Showing staving, side planks, sheer strake, knightsheads, insets for bobstay and jib stay irons. Courtesy of Allen Rawl.

will be transformed into a proper table of offsets, and then a set of line drawings to be used throughout the restoration process. We began fashioning the new stem piece from hardwood from Belize and new sheer strakes from my inventory of South American locust – beautiful, hard, durable wood. The new stem piece was clamped into place. We got out intermediate frames and began fitting them into place. A new stem knee was fashioned out of a large piece of purple heart wood from my inventory and was fitted with the new stem.

November 12 - 24. Warm and fair weather, absolutely perfect for boat building. The stem knees are fastened and fit beautifully. The upper transom plank has been fitted. The sheer strakes and top side planks were fitted amidships, where fresh water had gotten in around the roller chocks and rotted well into the uppermost topside planking. Hardwood was used for this purpose. With a full crew of eight workers we replaced several intermediate frames and gradually removed the beam clamps that needed replacing. We added temporary bracing to hold *Martha's* shape during the restoration. All remaining sheer strakes were fastened, as were the portside beam clamp pieces. The new hardwood breasthook is now fitted and fastened. Transom framing is complete. The interior of the hull is treated with fish oil and a wood preservative. With heavy weather in the forecast, the cover over the boat is now completely secure.

November 27. Quarter knees were added to enhance the integrity of the stern. The transom framing is a major improvement to the boat's

TOP: Side repair. October 1993. Courtesy of Allen Rawl.

BOTTOM: Upper and lower transom beams, deck beams, quarter knees, rudder shaft box, rudder shaft assembly, transom frames, transom planks, kick-up stern and stringer, beam clamp and chocks. Courtesy of Allen Rawl.

structure. Very hard rain this evening.

NOVEMBER 29 - December 1. Very cold. Deck beams are gotten out of Douglas fir planks. Approximately one-third of the fore-and-aft stringers port and starboard have been removed, as they were of questionable integrity. Deck beams going in steadily. A piece of hardwood was fashioned and fastened over the end grain of the deadwood. The stern post and shaft log of the yawl boat were removed due to rot.

DECEMBER 2 - 3. Warm and sunny. Most of the deck beams are in place, as are the half-beams and carlins. The rudder post housing is being made of juniper with rabbeted corners and through-fastened with drifts peened over clench rings. An old Dutchman that had been set into the keel many years ago looked a bit shaky, so we replaced it.

ABOVE: Deck beams and main hatch coaming. Showing clamps, chocks, Samson post, centerboard well, forward king plank, sheer strakes, quarter knees. Courtesy of Allen Rawl. OPPOSITE PAGE: author and Allen Rawl. December 1993.

DECEMBER 4. Heavy rain. The night's high winds collapsed the boat cover over the deck.

DECEMBER 7 - 10. Sunny and cold. We began serious work on the metal parts, namely the anchor windlass and steering wheel. Hatch framing and mast partners are being fitted. We started getting out the pieces for the strongback to be fitted midships. I contacted the Coast Guard inspector about a possible access hatch in the collision bulkhead, but the idea was not received favorably.

Of all the places I have experienced at boatyards, the Concord Point Lighthouse Park is the most beautiful and enchanting. We are constantly observed by ducks, geese, gulls, an early morning heron – and I'm sure the bald eagle sees us more than we see him. The water is alive with fish and the passing workboats and pleasure boats give the place an air of usefulness and necessity.

As to *Martha Lewis*, the pieces for the strongback are being fashioned and the hardwood mast partner assembly is being fastened, one piece at a time – these will be connected to the horizontal arms of the hanging knees that form the bracing at the mast step, partners and hull. The iron stern railing and chain plates are being inspected, repaired and cleaned. All metal parts will be sent for re-galvanizing. We have begun the arduous task of plugging and filling all the defects in the hull. The yawl boat is now in the Boat School for restoration.

ABOVE:
Sam Jones, master shipwright.
Hanging and standing knees
create an oval support
between strongback (mast
step) and mast partners.
Demonstrates side planking,
deck beams, intermediate
frames, bottom planks, chine
log. Both images courtesy of
Allen Rawl.

LEFT:
Samson post stepped on the
keel. Showing bottom planks,
stringers, stem knee, lower
breast hook.

DECEMBER 13. Drove to St. Michaels, Maryland to study *Rosie Parks* at the Maritime Museum. She is one of *Martha's* sister ships. I took notes, made drawings and photographed many of her fittings and details. I hope to share *Martha's* details with the Museum.

DECEMBER 14 - 15. The storm-damaged boat cover has been removed and today we are now building a new one, this time using wood trusses and reinforced plastic sheeting. We also began fitting the many chocks running fore and aft between the deck beams. These will support and act as nailers for the deck planking ends as they are nibbed into the margin piece. We fitted and fastened four hardwood lodging knees at each outboard corner of the main hatch framing, for strength and stiffness. We also sistered two backing blocks to the deck beams to support the aft roller chocks' knees.

Deck beams, half beam, main hatch coaming, centerboard well, keel, beam clamp, chocks, floor planks and stringers.
Courtesy of Allen Rawl.

DECEMBER 16 - 18. We are beginning on the fume-tight bulkhead, located just forward of the trunk cabin. This is one of two bulkheads required by the Coast Guard before they will issue a certificate to carry passengers. The second one is the water-tight collision bulkhead just forward of the mast.

DECEMBER 24 - 25. Cold and light snowfall. We took advantage of the crew's time off to pressure-spray the interior of the hull with a mixture of fish oil and an acceptable preservative, called copper-A-quinolate. The thirsty wood soaks up the fish oil.

DECEMBER 28. Yesterday the temperature did not rise above 20 degrees. Today is a bit warmer, with 3" of snow. We continue work on the collision bulkhead – the final layer of cedar planking, after a double membrane of 15-pound roofing paper, bedded in plastic roof cement attached to the first layer of diagonal planking. Dutchmen and plugs for the hull are made, but gluing must wait until the weather clears.

DECEMBER 29 - JANUARY 3. Cold, not enough warming to melt the snow. The collision bulkhead is finished. With the new hardwood stem, the bracing at the mast partners and forward bulkhead in place, *Martha* is becoming very stiff, stem to stern. Main hatch coamings are now fastened with traditional 3-part mortise joints at the corners. The aft hatch coamings are next. Metal railings are now altered to increase their

OPPOSITE PAGE:
Yawl boat with decay removed.
December 1993.
Courtesy Allen Rawl.

RIGHT:
Yawl boat inverted, repaired,
awaiting painting at
Havre de Grace
Wooden Boat School.
Notice engine cooling pipes.
April 1994.
Courtesy Allen Rawl.

BELOW:
Yawl boat on davits.
Chestertown. 2002.
Courtesy Elizabeth Rawl.

height above the deck to 38" Coast Guard specifications. At the Boat School, lines for the yawl boat have been taken and it is now stripped of all decayed parts – more serious than we thought.

JANUARY 5 - 7. Very cold, well below freezing. We are milling stock for rails and centerboard and pieces for a new keel and frames for the yawl boat. The 6-cylinder gasoline winder engine was started, then partially disassembled for inspection. We re-fastened the centerboard well box with galvanized boat nails and began shaping the new hardwood rudder post and Douglas fir piece for the king plank.

JANUARY 8. Not above freezing all day. Yesterday's wind and last night's light snow have frozen and crystallized into a beautiful wintry scene at Concord Point. The crew defies the cold and actually appreciates the beauty. The kingplank is ready for fastening, along with the rudder post. The log, upper and rub rails are milled to size and a crew is milling stock for the frames, keel and bottom planking for the yawl boat.

JANUARY 10 - 11. Frozen rain has caused slippery conditions. Our shipsmith is beginning work on the stern davits and rudder gudgeon and pintle. We fitted the king plank, painted and prepared it for bedding and fastening. The rudder post is fastened to the rudder block. We milled the rub rail sections, hollowed the back side and painted them. They need only to be fitted and fastened. The first attempt to extract the bottom plank fasteners on the port side showed them to have some age, but to be relatively sound.

JANUARY 12 - 13. Rain and warming. The king plank is thoroughly fastened and looks massive without the adjacent deck planking. All of the galvanized tie rods are firmly bolted in place, connecting the last three beams to the transom beam. On the port side, at the chine, midship, we cut out the "punky" ends of the bottom hull planking where the dredge cable has taken its toll. We let in a longitudinal piece of hardwood to fill in and strengthen this area. We are spot-refastening the bottom planking with 4" galvanized wood screws in a pattern alternate to the existing fasteners. There is enough warming to allow gluing of the plugs in the hull planking, hatch coamings and king planks. Coast Guard has approved the drawings for the aluminum fuel tanks and piping system.

JANUARY 14. Warm and drizzly, then turning cold. The aft hatch, just forward of the trunk cabin, was fitted with coamings, with care for proper drainage, since the coaming on the after side is attached to the forward side of the cabin. We began seizing the seam where the bottom planking joins the keel. After refastening the bottom, we will re-caulk this seam. The first vertical plank, called staving, aft of the stem, was fitted and fastened and the planks of hardwood for the new centerboard were dressed and edge-fitted. The inside of the hull was cleaned again and a small Dutchman fitted on the port side, forward, where the chine log meets the stem.

JANUARY 15. Bitter cold: 10 degrees with a wind chill of -30 degrees. We paused work at the yard.

JANUARY 17. Thermometer in the mid-teens with 3" of snow. The snow turned to rain by evening, then to frozen rain. Nonetheless, we began serious re-fastening of the bottom planks on the port side. We are fitting staving at the bow. The aft hatch coaming has been fastened into place and two hatch cover beams were shaped and fitted. Snow found its way into the stem of *Martha's* hull.

January 1994 weather in Havre de Grace. Collapsed boat cover.
Courtesy of Allen Rawl.

Reconstructed bow. Showing stem, sheer strake, collision bulkhead, side planking, staving, keel shoe, knightheads. Courtesy of Allen Rawl.

JANUARY 18 - 21. Bitter cold. Morning low on the 19th was -11 degrees with a wind chill of -41 degrees. The cover over the skipjack has collapsed under the weight of the snow. We moved some equipment into the Boat School. The combined crews fastened several side-frames and bottom-frames. They stripped the lower side-planking.

JANUARY 22 - 23. Warmer and relatively pleasant. The entire crew turned out to repair the cover over *Martha*. By mid-afternoon we were back under cover and secure. We made a proper stairway from the ground to the deck and placed plywood sheets over some of the deck beams to allow visitors to come aboard.

On the 23rd we held a reception, attended by sixty persons, all related by their connection to *Martha Lewis*.

JANUARY 24 - 25. Warm and sunny. We continued re-fastening *Martha's* bottom planking. Fitted and fastened some of the topside planking at the bow and began fastening the new centerboard pieces with galvanized steel drifts. We began shaping the new bowsprit from a Douglas fir timber.

JANUARY 26 - 31. Very cold, with high winds, freezing rain and snow. We painted the top of the deck structure in preparation for the new deck. We will use North Carolina juniper (American white cedar) for the deck. We will draw from our stock of South American locust for the covering boards, since there is not enough juniper. This is heavier, but stronger, and very durable. The lower part of the new stem piece was shaped by adze and planer and notches have been cut to let in the bobstay irons. We have finished placing approximately 1,400 new fasteners in the bottom planking and have made over 3,000 wood plugs to fill in behind the fasteners, before fairing the bottom and deck.

FEBRUARY 2 - 5. Our Coast Guard inspector approved our refastening of the bottom planking, collision bulkhead, fume-tight bulkhead, midships strongback, transom framing and the deck structure. We have finished plugging the knots and cutting the outguage of decking planks to create a caulking seam. The hardwood covering board has been fitted, bedded and fastened with a proper hooked-scarf joint. We are laying the new deck forward, where the kingplank meets the bow. In the metal shop on site, we are restoring the dredge roller chocks, which are probably original to the boat. We continue laying the new deck, restoring the iron work and fashioning a new gammon iron for the bowsprit.

New deck. Showing covering board, margin piece, nibbed deck planking, king plank, and forepeak hatch opening.
Courtesy Allen Rawl.

FEBRUARY 6 - 13. High winds, freezing rain and ice, sleet and snow greatly delay our work. We laid the last deck plank. We cleaned off the deck and began caulking the plank seams. At the Boat School, the keel, stern post and stem knee have been temporarily fastened. Bottom planking has begun and many plugs were cut to fill in behind the deck and hull fasteners.

FEBRUARY 15 - 16. We began preparing *Martha's* bulwarks for re-installation. They are mostly oak or heart pine and very heavy. The warmer weather does wonders for the moral of the crew. At the transom the log (toe) rail pattern was made – an elliptical curve, as it rounds the corner, and several pieces were fashioned and fastened. The port-side bulwarks were fitted to the new covering board and fastened in place. We have begun deck caulking.

Refitting the bulwarks. February 1994. Courtesy of Allen Rawl.

FEBRUARY 17 - 19. Several pieces of the transom were replaced or reefed and splined. Starboard bulwarks were quickly fitted and fastened. I made a pattern for the steel cable guards at the chine, near the transom – they will have to be heated and edge-set to the proper shape. The original steel roller chocks have been separated from their metal plates and braces – added during her mid-life – and we are fitting hardwood knees very similar to those she originally wore. The bowsprit is painted and varnished and nearly ready for stepping.

FEBRUARY 21 - 25. Some snow and then hard rain. The original steering box was cleaned and placed on the quarter deck and no alterations were necessary. We began work on the mast that was taken out of the boat last fall. Other than the rot at the heel, it appears to be a fine piece of Douglas fir. Although shorter than before, after cutting off the rot, we will step it and shorten up the rig and sails for temporary use, until we can purchase new spar timber from Oregon. At the Concord Point Sail Loft the sails were restored in two days. They needed re-stitching throughout, new grommets and most of the bolt ropes re-sewn.

Dredge winder. Tilghman Island. September 1993. Courtesy Allen Rawl.

FEBRUARY 26 - 27. We begin restoration of the dredge winders. We added bolsters at the hounds of the mast, as the shoulders showed signs of deterioration. The bolsters will help support the standing rigging.

Steering gear assembly. September 1993.
Courtesy Allen Rawl.

Rigging has been sorted and all the blocks repaired or discarded for replacement. The push boat's bottom is now two-thirds planked and the caulking is begun. The hardwood frames, keel and bottom planking will make her a stiff little work boat.

February 28. Twelve degrees at the yard. In the metal shop we are fabricating the stanchions for the rail forward of the traditional stern railing, as required by the Coast Guard. These will be used when carrying passengers and detached when we are dredging. I picked up the aluminum fuel tanks from the molding shop.

March 1. Warming. We caulked the deck seams and the keel rabbet. A fairlead was let into the bowsprit. The mast was scraped and the first of many coats of oil solution was applied. Davit braces and the jib sheet traveler were restored.

March 2 - 3. High winds, snow and sleet forced us to close the yard.

March 4 - 8. Warming and cloudy, turning to rain. Deck seam caulking continues and we are beginning to pay the seams with pitch. The fancy rail is being fitted. A crew was assembled to cut, fit and fasten the stainless steel ice sheathing. We are prepping the trunk cabin for paint and are welding the frame for the forepeak hatch. Fuel tank pressure test passed Coast Guard inspection.

March 9 - 10. Yard closed due to low temperatures, sleet and wind-driven rain.

MARCH 11 - 15. The deck was scraped to remove excess pitch from the seams. We scarfed a new piece of fir on the end of the broken boom, deciding on a clothes-pin scarf for maximum strength. The days were spent sanding and painting the topsides, wheel box, winder engine cover, headrails and trunk cabin. Hull painting is finished. Mast wedges were fashioned and set in place. The fuel tanks were positioned below deck at each quarter. A new housing is made for the centerboard deck sheave. The ironwork began arriving from the galvanizing plant in Baltimore.

MARCH 16 - 17. Cold, but beautiful weather. We began running pipes and valves from the fuel tank. Dredge rollers are restored to working condition and are left ungalvanized. They and their brackets are clamped in place. The fancy rail is in place. The cutwater is fitted and fastened in place. Bobstay irons at the stem and the chainplates are fitted and fastened. The transponder for the depth finder is reinstalled in its through-hull fitting. Iron strapping is secured to the centerboard by rivets. Burlap is placed in the hull and soaked with water to swell the planking. The load water line is marked on the hull.

MARCH 18 - 19. Snow flurries, then clearing. The rudder is set in place, now that the gudgeon has been fastened to the stern post and the pintle fastened to the rudder. The gammoning iron is mounted over the bowsprit and fastened to the stem piece below. All straps and lifting irons have been attached to the centerboard. A second coat of paint has been applied to the deck and the topsides are nearly finished. We are paying the bottom planking seams with seam compound and wax rendered from hydrogenated fish oil. The stern pipe railings are installed, as are cable guards of half-oval galvanized steel. The fuel supply manifold has been constructed just forward of the rudder post housing, between the two fuel tanks.

MARCH 20 - 23. The stainless steel sheathing was cleaned, then primed, in preparation for painting. The boot top and head at the sheer are painted, as are the wheel box and push block. The new white oak davit board, deck plates and main sheet traveler are installed. The beautiful steering wheel is repainted. Two screw-out deck vents are installed to allow for proper ventilation in the fore peak.

MARCH 24 - 25. Whisker stays are secured to the bowsprit and bulwarks. The name of the vessel and hailing port are being painted on the transom. Bilge pumps are installed and electrical wiring and piping are connected. The mast hoops have been restored or replaced and now are slid onto the mast. Cleats are attached to the mast and boom, made from scrap pieces of the oak knight heads we removed earlier. Seam paying is now complete. Rigging is set up on the mast. We removed the weather cover over the boat. Trail boards and name boards are attached. We began cleaning the yard.

New home port. March 1994.

MARCH 26. Clear and sunny. Early this morning we attached the eagle figure-head to the end of the cutwater. The Aberdeen Proving Ground crew with two cranes and two flatbed trailers, lifted *Martha* from her cradle, hauled her through town to Tydings Marina and there, at approximately 0730 set her quietly back into the water, where she belongs. The mast was stepped and temporary shrouds and stays set up, the winders and engines set in their places on the deck. She leaked very little for a cross-planked skipjack.

Top: Relaunch day at Concord Point.

Bottom: Relaunch day with assist by equipment and crew of Aberdeen Proving Grounds. March 26, 1994.

After the relaunching, until April 14, *Martha Lewis* was prepared for sailing. Standing and running rigging were set up in a permanent fashion, the yawl boat restoration was completed and the jib club and main boom were varnished. A new mainsail club was fashioned. The jib-sheet block, typical to only Chesapeake skipjacks, was fashioned so all the sheet ran forward of the mast, through a pennant from the hounds and belayed to a pin on the port sheer-pole. The traditional gold ball at the mast head signified that the boat was "complete and paid for." The yawl boat engine was installed and controls and cooling hoses completed. Ballast racks were installed in *Martha* midships and safety rails and stanchions were placed on her bulwarks.

Sea trials were successful on April 23, 1994.

Martha Lewis under power. April 1995. Courtesy Elizabeth Rawl.

Postscript

Since our final on-board inspection, we have had our Certificate revised to allow us to carry 34 persons on all lakes, bays and sounds, with the one-mile-of-shore restriction lifted. We will work to raise funds for a hydrostatic and stability study completed to help the Coast Guard determine *Martha's* true limitations.

Martha seems to be off to a grand beginning. There is a lot of local interest. Dr. George has gifted her to posterity and she will operate under the direction of the Chesapeake Heritage Conservancy, in alliance with the Havre de Grace Maritime Museum. My wife, Elizabeth, and I will manage her through our company, Allen C. Rawl, Incorporated. She is a good boat and already has the respect of many knowledgeable Chesapeake Bay sailors, historians and enthusiasts.

- *Allen C. Rawl*

SKIPJACK
MARTHA LEWIS
1955

RESTORATION   1994

CONSTRUCTION PLAN
AND SECTIONS
by— ALLEN C. RAWL, INCORPORATED
for
THE SKIPJACK MARTHA LEWIS , INC.
AND
THE HAVRE de GRACE MARITIME MUSEUM

DRAWN BY: *AcRawl*   APRIL 17,1994   TRACED BY: T.M.R.

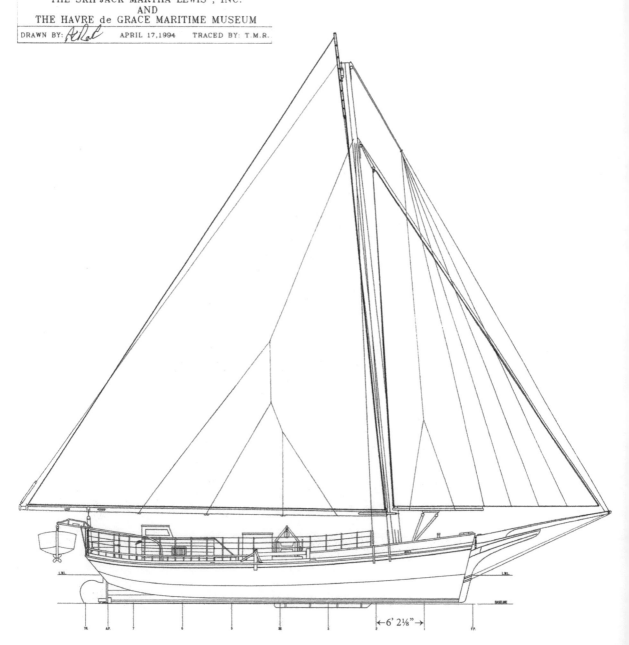

← 6' 2⅛" →

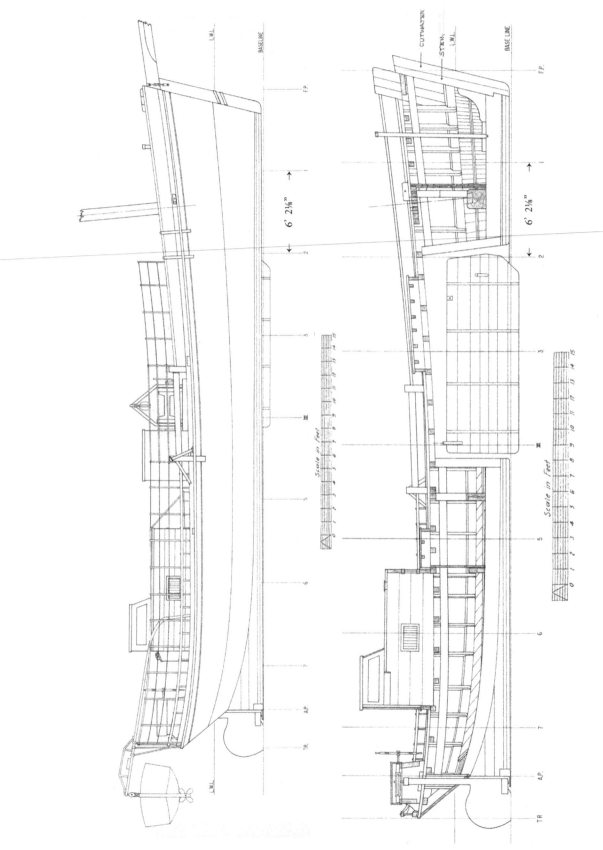

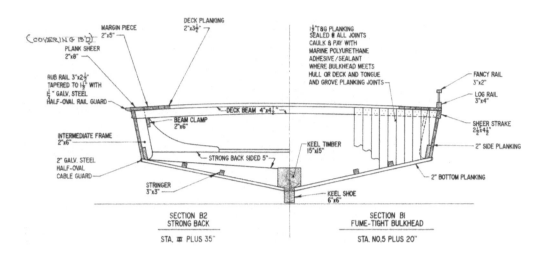

SECTION B2
STRONG BACK

STA. III PLUS 35"

SECTION B1
FUME-TIGHT BULKHEAD

STA. NO.5 PLUS 20"

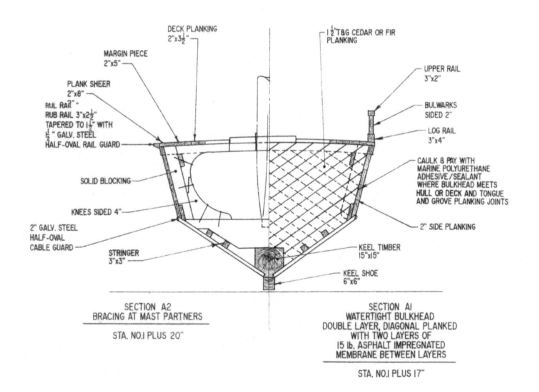

SECTION A2
BRACING AT MAST PARTNERS

STA. NO.I PLUS 20"

SECTION AI
WATERTIGHT BULKHEAD
DOUBLE LAYER, DIAGONAL PLANKED
WITH TWO LAYERS OF
15 lb. ASPHALT IMPREGNATED
MEMBRANE BETWEEN LAYERS

STA. NO.I PLUS 17"

Scale in Feet

FP.

6' 2⅛"

QUARTER KNEE

TRANSOM BR.

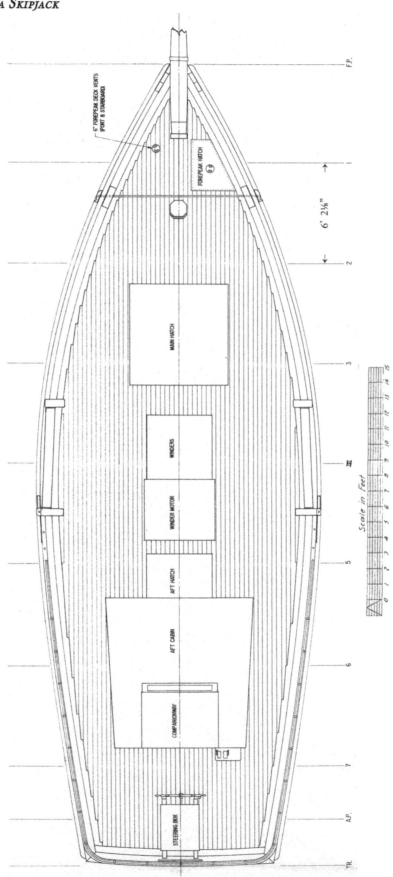

Afterword

The year that we reconstructed *Martha Lewis*, she missed her first oyster season. I rued this because of my belief that that her survival depended on her continuing the work she was meant to do. That year the State of Maryland was still trying to restore the oyster population by transplanting young oysters called spat from state planting beds to other controlled areas farther up the Bay. We were accepted into the program and were instructed by the Division of Natural Resources where and how many bushels to dredge. The state beds were north of Smith Island in Kedges Strait, so we sailed down to Crisfield that spring, and docked at the City pier. The night before our work was to begin there was a ferocious storm from the northwest with high winds and driving rain.

We spent a very rough night on board with the boat thumping up against the old tires hanging from the dock. Below decks we were curled up in sleeping bags, trying to listen to the boat through the screaming of the wind. Her creaking and banging and flapping of her rigging went on all night long. No one slept. We knew *Martha* wouldn't break, but she still took a beating. The next morning we found gouges and scrapes all along the lee rail, but no serious trouble.

Once the weather cleared, we motored out to the dredge site and began the back-breaking task of dredging old shells covered with spat and stacking them as high as we could over the entire deck. Plywood boards along the gunnels allowed us to shovel tons of shell onto the boat until her freeboard slowly sank, and we had taken on our maximum load. We pushed slowly up the Bay, and carried the shell to the Choptank River where, among marked buoys on open water, we shoveled them over the side. Our fledgling crew didn't earn much money for *Martha's* upkeep that day, but we were all satisfied to have hauled oysters in our first year.

With oyster populations depleted by overfishing and two parasites called MSX and Dermo, most of the remaining skipjacks cannot support themselves by dredging. Many have sought shelter in 501(c)(3) corpora-

Spatting in Kedges Straits. May 1994.
Note spatting boards in place around the deck.

tions where deductible donations are allowed for their maintenance. As educational venues, they are used to teach adults and school children about the history and health of the Chesapeake Bay.

Even with this relief, carrying passengers adds additional responsibilities and costs. The Coast Guard is very vigilant when it comes to ensuring the safety of passengers. It mandates frequent inspections and periodic replacement of planking and beams. In addition, the need for paid crews, fuel, paint, sails, and insurance force costs into the many tens of thousands of dollars per year. To keep *Martha* afloat, a team of dedicated volunteers is essential to write grants, solicit donations, find corporate sponsors, organize fund-raising events and passenger trips, and to fund an endowment.

In 1994 I donated *Martha Lewis* to the non-profit Chesapeake Heritage Conservancy based in Havre de Grace, Maryland. Since then a long list of dedicated volunteers have maintained her, worked her, and used her for her new educational mission.

Beginning in 1994 *Martha's* story has really been their story, to be told by them in their own way.

Wooden boats always deteriorate. They constantly fall prey to the elements. In 2013 *Martha Lewis* underwent repairs at a yard in Baltimore. When she was unable to adequately swell her planks on re-entering the water, she was placed in dry-dock, where she remains as of this writing. The longer she rests there, even under cover, the greater the possibility that she will grow old, fall into ruin, and pass the way of so many others of her kind into the fog of history.

Appendix A

A Glossary of Major Components of the Chesapeake Bay Skipjack *Martha Lewis*

Note: Most of these definitions were either written or edited by Allen Rawl, without whom this list would not have been attempted. Terms used in a definition and also defined in this glossary have been *italicized*. For scantlings (measurements) please refer to the construction profiles.

===

Anchor windlass – A manually operated apparatus with a pair of drums, port and starboard, also known as gypsies, mounted on the aft face of the Samson post, the purpose of which is to raise the anchor, haul a dock line or other similar task.

Backing block – A fore and aft member, installed between deck beams, centered on the inner edge of the deck margin piece to serve as "backing" for fastening the nibbed ends of the deck planking as necessary. At the *forepeak* the backing block angles toward the *stem piece* and is called a beam shelf.

Beam clamp – A longitudinal strake, running from transom to stem, fastened to the inside face of the hull frames, under and supporting the deck beams.

Bobstay – A chain extending from a steel band at the outer end of the bowsprit to a *bobstay iron*, which counteracts the lifting force of the forestay.

Bobstay iron – A steel strap, fitted to and let into the leading edge the stem, below the load water line, to which the lower end of the bobstay is attached.

Bolster – The shoulder of the *hounds*, resting atop the cheek piece, designed to prevent chafing by shrouds and stays that are looped over the mast.

Boot top – Painted stripe at the load water line.

BOWSPRIT – A spar which projects forward from the stem, the purpose of which is to extend the head rigging to counteract the effect of the main sail, thereby keeping the sail arrangement in balance.

BOWSPRIT GUY / BOWSPRIT SHROUD – A chain that extends from a steel band at the outer end of the bowsprit, port and starboard, to an eyebolt in the bulwark forward of the mast chain plates providing lateral support to the bowsprit.

BURTON TACKLE – A general purpose tackle with two blocks, usually rigged aloft, for lifting cargo or any item requiring a mechanical advantage; on a skipjack, often to lift the mainsail boom at the jaws.

BREAST HOOK – A triangular wood block, preferably from a natural crook of a tree, mounted behind the stem, just below the deck, to strengthen the bow framing.

BULWARK – Raised woodwork running along each side of the deck edge, attached to a log *rail* which is mounted on the covering board, and capped by a top *rail*. Serves to keep seas from flooding the deck and to prevent cargo and/or crew from falling or being washed overboard.

CABIN SOLE – The floor of the trunk cabin, supported by small, thwartship beams, extending to the chine logs.

CARLIN – A fore and aft beam mitered between main thwartship deck beams to create a hatch opening or to reinforce the deck framing. Half beams are mitered into the carlin's outboard edge.

CAULKING – The process of filling and tightening hull or deck planks by driving one strand of cotton into the back of the caulking seam followed by one or more (as required) strands of rolled, tarred oakum, set tightly using a caulking iron and mallet. The seam is then painted and when dry, *payed* with seam compound of choice. When caulking is removed, it is "reefed out". *Martha's* side and deck caulking seams are 2/3 of the plank's depth at the outguage, while the inguage 1/3 is butted. When seams are deemed too wide to hold caulking, additional strips or splines are wedged lengthwise in the deepest part of the seams, and then the caulking is applied.

CENTERBOARD – A device to increase the area of lateral resistance when a boat is sailing to windward and to prevent excessive leeway. Constructed of hardwood planks, edge-drifted, all stiffened by metal bands on either side of the assembly. It travels and pivots, inside the centerboard trunk on a pin near the forward end of the board where there is a vertical slot (in lieu of a hole), to allow the board to rise in the event of striking an underwater object, or running aground. Tackle, to provide mechanical advantage for raising and lowering the board, consists of a lanyard which is attached to a steel fitting located at the upper, aft corner of the board which is led over a sheave mounted in the deck, then continues on to a fairlead (or sheave) mounted on the forward edge of the aft cabin. Thereafter, the lanyard is attached to a rope block tackle that terminates at the aft end of the cabin where the fall is belayed to a cleat mounted on the cabin top. This allows the operator of the boat to control the depth of the centerboard while *Martha* is moored or underway.

CENTERBOARD TRUNK – A water-tight planked box housing the centerboard, within the confines of the forward compartment, with posts at each end, fastened to rails (logs) atop the keel, which itself provides a 4" slot as an opening for the centerboard to move up or down.

CHAIN PLATE – A galvanized strap vertically oriented on either side of the hull, bolted through the topside planks to a frame or inside blocking. Located just aft of the mast, the chain plate serves as an anchor for each of the mast shrouds. The rub

rail is fastened over the chain plate.

CHINE – The line of intersection where the topside planking meets the bottom planking, running fore and aft the entire length of the ship.

CHINE LOG – A heavy plank which runs from the aft face of the mid stem to the lower transom frame. This supports the frames, the lowest side plank and the outboard ends of the bottom planks. Toward the stern, the chine log is bent upward and inward, eventually meeting the lower transom beam.

CHOCK – A block of wood to connect or reinforce joining pieces, or as filling pieces. Chocks are mortised between deck beams just above the clamps so support deck planking.

CLUB – A substantial spar, fairly unique to *Martha Lewis*, laced to the luff of the head of the mainsail, with the main *halyard* attached just above its midpoint. The club gives rigidity to the luff above the *hounds* and allows the sail to be raised above the head of the mast. A downhaul at its foot assures that it remain vertical, and assists in lowering the mainsail.

COAMING (HATCH) – A raised border around a hatch opening to prevent water on deck from running below. Mounted on and attached directly to deck beam and carlin, the coaming also serves to restore the strength to these members compromised by cutting the opening for the hatch.

COVERING BOARD – Planks, on skipjacks, the thickness of deck planking, running fore and aft, defining the deck edge, resting on the deck beams and frame heads. Also called a "plank shear."

CUTWATER – Curved board, essentially a triangle, fastened to the stem and the long head, serving its namesake purpose, also contributing to the elegant shape of the clipper bow peculiar to skipjacks.

DAVITS (BOAT) – Galvanized steel rods, port and starboard, anchored to the log rail, abreast the aft cabin curving upward and astern, extending outboard of the transom sufficient to support the yawl boat and its tackle. Davits are further reinforced by three triangulated, galvanized rods at each quarter to afford vertical support as well as to prevent shifting. A wood plank known as a "davit board" is bolted athwartships atop the davits outboard from the transom serving to stablize the davit assembly, and as a secure platform for tending the push boat and reefing the main sail.

DEADWOOD – An assembly of wood timbers, to fill in the triangular space aft between the upturned keel and the keel shoe. The exposed end-grain of the deadwood is protected by a vertical wood plate.

DECK – Skipjacks have only one deck, called a flush, weather deck, with minimal sheer. Areas of the deck may be called foredeck, midship and quarter deck, referring to relative location only.

DECK BEAM – A thwartship timber, supporting the deck planking, bolted to and resting on the beam clamps. Beams serve as ties or struts to connect the vessel's sides. They may not necessarily meet with or be connected to the hull frames.

DRIFTS – Steel rods used to connect wooden members where threaded bolts are not practical. The ends of drifts, as an alternative to threaded nuts, may be secured with clench rings.

DUTCHMAN – Wood block let into a mortise, glued and/or mechanically fastened, then fayed to the surrounding surface. Used to repair an area where surface wood has been compromised due to rot or other damage. A wood plug is similar, but round to fill (for example) the void of recessed fastenings.

FOREPEAK – Forward-most extent of the hull.

FRAME – A vertical, member supporting the side hull planking. On skipjacks these are called intermediate frames at all points except at the strongback and mast partner assembly. The frame is notched over the chine log and bolted to the outboard side of the *clamp*. The transom also has frames between the upper and lower *transom beams*, which support the transom planks.

GAMMON IRON – A galvanized, steel band which secures, by means of a threaded rod and turnbuckle arrangement, the bowsprit to the head of the stem.

HANK – One of a series of rings securing the luff of the jib to its stay.

HATCH – An opening in the deck structure to allow access into a compartment below. *Martha* has three hatch openings in her deck: 1) the smaller aft hatch, located between the trunk cabin and the *winders*, which provides access to the aft end of the main hold; 2) the main hatch or cargo hatch between the winders and the mast; 3) the forepeak hatch allowing access to the forepeak, located forward of the mast, starboard side, fitted with an aluminum plate, flush with the deck, which is required by the U.S. Coast Guard to be secured while underway. Pipe berths for the crew are constructed on the sides of the forward hull and are accessed through the main hatch.

HEADRAILS – Paired outboard wood rails, which extend from the forward bulwark assembly to the longhead just behind the figurehead. They are cross-braced by a thwartship plank, secured to the longhead forward of the stem. A galvanized, steel rod passes between the head rails to complete the assemblage.

HEADSTAY – The most forward part of the standing rigging. The wire rope support tying the end of the bowsprit and the mast head.

HOOD-END – End of hull and bulwark plank, which terminate at the stem or stern rabbet.

HORSE – A steel rod to which a *traveler* may be attached. The jib horse is a straight rod passing through the bulwarks just forward of the mast. The main horse is a shorter, elongated U-shaped rod behind the *steering gear* box, mounted to the deck, with under-deck blocking.

HOUNDS – Projection at either side of the mast at a point approximately 85% above the deck, consisting of a cheek piece and bolsters, which serve as a fairlead over which the mast shrouds and stays are led in pairs. Also, the attachment points for the jib halyard block, main *la-*

zy-jack lines, and boom lift *burton tackle.*

ICE SHEATHING – Stainless steel plating along the chine, several inches above and below the load water line to protect the wood members from being damaged by ice.

JIB SAIL – A triangular, fore-and-aft sail set on the jib stay by a series of *hanks*, leading from the bowsprit to the hounds of the mast, arranged with four *reef points.*

JIB SAIL RIGGING – Consists of several components: 1) the halyard, a line used for hoisting and lowering the sail; 2) the jib sheet, a line used to control the foot of the sail. On a shipjack, in lieu of attaching to the clew, the jib sheet is attached to the jib club, a substantial wood pole laced to the after foot of the sail. 3) Peculiar to skipjacks, the jib sheet is then led through a "jib sheet block". 4) This block is connected to an arrangement known as a *horse* and *traveler* just forward of the mast, then led up to a pendant block which is suspended from the hounds. The fall is then led to a belaying pin on a sheer pole mounted on the port shrouds. This arrangement allows the jib sail to be mostly self-tending; *lazy-jacks* are the merging of four lines attached to the foot of the sail, into one line that is attached to a *spectacle iron*, which travels along the head stay and is controlled by a line led to a block at the mast head then to a belaying point on the port sheer pole.

JIB STAY – Part of the standing rigging. A wire rope, just behind the forestay, on which the jib-*hanks* travel as the jib sail is raised or lowered. Looped over the mast at the hounds, it runs to the outer end of the bowsprit which is pierced with a built-in sheave. Through this the jib stay is led to the *jib-stay iron* at the stem.

JIB STAY IRON – A steel strap, fitted to and let into the leading edge the stem, below the load water line just above the bob stay iron, to which the lower end of the jib stay is attached.

KEEL RABBET – A shoulder or recess to receive the bottom planking and to protect its end grain. Traditionally, on skipjacks, the rabbet is on the bottom, outer corners, leaving the keel timber completely inside the hull structure.

KEEL SHOE – A longitudinal timber, or build-up of layers, fastened to the bottom of the keel timber the entire length of the keel pierced by the center-board shaft. Depending upon the material from which it is made, this piece can serve as a "worm-shoe", made of soft wood to attract marine bores or a "false-keel", made of hardwood to provide better protection for grounding, etc. In either case, the keel shoe is effectively a sacrificial piece. At Wingate, the keel shoe was bolted through the keel, and was called the "skag." An additional sacrificial layer was added beneath it called the "worm strip" or "wear strip".

KEEL TIMBER – The main center-line structural member, running fore and aft along the bottom of the boat, also known as the "backbone," on which rests the stem at the forward end and the sternpost/transom assembly aft. It is selected from a tree with a bend, providing for a rising of the keel toward the stern. Local parlance calls the keel a keelson, since it is primarily internal to the hull.

KICK-UP BOTTOM – A few feet forward of the transom, the chevroned bottom planking is terminated on a beam between the keel and the chine log. Fore-and-aft planking is then continued to the lower transom beam.

KING PLANK – An (optional) piece of the deck structure, usually thicker than the deck planking, usually several feet in width, extending along the center line of the deck from bow to stern, interrupted by the hatches and cabin. The mast pierces the king plank.

KNEES – Reinforcements, preferably fashioned from burley pieces of tree trunk or natural grown timbers, with "body" and "arm" at various angles, used to reinforce the intersections of beams or timbers. Named for the position in which they are attached: hanging knees are attached vertically to top and side; standing knees attached vertically to bottom and side: lodging knees are attached horizontally at the intersection of horizontal members. Lodging knees include the quarter knees between the upper transom beams and the sheer strakes, and the four knees reinforcing the *carlins* and *deck beams* at the outboard corners of the trunk cabin. The heavy stem knee (standing) reinforces the intersection of the keel and stem.

KNIGHTHEADS – The first vertical timbers on either side of the stem. Standing above the deck, they form the opening for the bowsprit, the head of the stem itself forming the actual seat. Bulwark planking is fastened to the outboard surface of the knightheads.

LAZYJACK – One of several lines, attached to either the foot of a sail or under a boom, or club, that merge into one line which is led aloft to a designated point, the purpose of which is to keep the sail from falling (on deck) when lowering and for ease of stowing.

LONGHEAD – A horizontal piece, fastened with drifts to the leading edge of the stem, beneath the bowsprit as the upper portion of the cutwater. The longhead does not support the bowsprit.

MAINSAIL – A triangular sail, the largest of the two sails, the luff of which is attached to, and travels vertically on the mast by a series of *mast hoops*. The foot of the sail is laced to the mainsail boom by a small diameter rope. The mainsail is arranged with four reef points. The skipjack mainsail is called a leg o'mutton sail, due to its shape.

MAINSAIL RIGGING – Consists of several component is: 1) the halyard is belayed to a cleat on the starboard side of the mast; 2) the *sheet* and sheet tackle provide the mechanical advantage needed for one or two crew to control the position of the mainsail and boom. The upper block is secured to the boom by means of a bale. The lower block, fitted with a *traveler*, is connected to a *horse* mounted on the deck just abaft the wheel box. The fall is belayed to a cleat on the port side of the wheel box; 3) the mainsail *lazyjacks* are four lines led under the mainsail boom, which merge into one line on each side that leads to a block at the hounds. Each fall is belayed to a cleat on its respective side of the boom; 4) the *topping lift* is a line from the outer end of the boom to a tackle at the head of the mast. Its fall is belayed to a pin on the starboard sheer pole at mast shrouds; 5) the boom lift (at jaws) provides working clearance, and is rigged with a *burton tackle*, belayed to a pin on the starboard sheer pole at the mast shrouds.

MANIFOLD (FUEL SUPPLY) – Also known as a distribution box, fitted with valves into which a number of fuel lines are led to control the path of fuel from tank or pump to engine or other machinery.

MARGIN PIECE (OR NIBBING STRAKE) – The longitudinal plank just inboard from the covering board, notched to receive the nibbed (tapered) ends of the deck planking. The process is called nibbing.

MAST HOOP – One of a series of laminated oak rings to which the luff of the mainsail is secured and which encircle and slide up and down the mast below the hounds as the sail is set or taken in.

MAST PARTNER ASSEMBLY – Wood blocks, let in between two beams to surround and support the mast where it passes through the deck. At the chine, standing knees are joined to hanging knees from the deck beams, and these join with the mast partners to create a continuous and substantial oval support for the mast.

Mast step – There is a large timber or strong-back mounted athwartships over the keel. At midship there is a mortise into which the tenon at the heel of the mast is <u>stepped</u>.

Mast wedges – Tapered pieces of wood driven around the mast to confine the mast between the partners. These are removed for "airing out" in the summer to prevent rot.

Pay – To run pitch, resin or seam compound into planking seams to complete the operation of *caulking*. (As in "*pay* a caulked seam")

Pendant block – A block seized to the lower end of a pendant, through which a line is led to a belaying station on deck.

Push block – A wood block secured to the transom, at the centerline, just below the deck edge to receive the stem of the yawl boat when positioned to push the main boat. Also called a jig or skeg.

Quarter Knee – See Knee

Rail – A long wood timber or a steel rod (bar). On most skipjacks, from the dredge rollers forward, there is a bottom or <u>log rail</u> under the bulwarks, and a top or <u>upper rail</u> directly atop the bulwarks. Astern, from the dredge rollers aft,

around the transom to the roller on the opposite side of the boat is another log (or bottom) rail, used as the seat for galvanized stanchions. The stanchions support the wood <u>fancy rail</u>. Above the fancy rail is a multiple rail assembly of stainless steel, called the <u>safety rail</u>, which extends to a height of about three feet. This rail is required on a vessel certified by the U.S. Coast Guard to carry passengers. It extends from the quarter deck forward to a point abaft the mast shrouds to define the limits of passenger encroachment. Completely surrounding the vessel, below the deck edge, is the <u>rub rail</u>, covered near the rollers by half-oval straps of stainless steel.

Reef knot – A knot used to make the lines fast at a reef point tied as a square knot bighted to form a single-slip, which allows the knot to be released by simply pulling the bighted end.

Reef point – An arrangement used to reduce the amount of sail exposed to the wind consisting of a grommet, one of several along a line at a given height through which a small line is passed of sufficient length to run under the foot of a sail. Its two ends are knotted together over the gathered canvas, finishing with a *reef knot*.

Reef tackle – A system to assist

in reefing the mainsail at each level, consisting of a cringle sewn into the leach of the sail to which a line is bent leading through a cheek-block on one side of the boom, then led forward and belayed to a cleat on the same side.

ROLLER CHOCK – A standing "knee", sometimes called roller stanchion, supporting the roller axle. The aft chock has galvanized struts inboard to the deck, outboard to the margin piece and aft to the log rail. Near the top of the aft chock is the bearing point for the vertical roller.

ROLLER, HORIZONTAL (DREDGE) – A steel, tubular piece, the purpose of which is to lead the oyster dredge cable overboard without chafing the deck or rail when dredging.

ROLLER, VERTICAL. (DREDGE) – An additional roller, raked aft, smaller than the horizontal roller. This serves to keep the dredge cable from traveling beyond and off of the after end of the horizontal roller when dredging. Its axle is supported by the aft roller knee and the rub rail.

RUDDER – A devise used for steering and maneuvering a boat or ship, consisting of two basic parts: a post and a blade. The post is a heavy wooden rot fitted with hardware at the head to which the *steering gear* is attached. The bottom is fitted with hardware including a pin (pintle), which fits into a corresponding socket (gudgeon) in the steel rudder hinge which is mounted to the lower, aft end of the keel shoe. A second gudgeon and pintle assembly, midway up the rudder post, is bolted to the *deadwood*. This assembly supports the entire weight of the rudder and allows it to pivot. The blade is built-up of several pieces of wood, edge-drifted to each other and into the post to the desired width and shape; it is usually tapered and rounded at the after end to continue the fair lines of the vessel.

RUDDER SHAFT ASSEMBLY – A blocked support for the rudder between the deck and the lower transom, including an intermediary box to keep out sea water.

SAMSON POST OR "KING POST" – A stout vertical timber stepped onto the keel, fastened to one of the deck beams. The heel of the bowsprit abuts the post and on the aft face the anchor windlass is mounted.

SCARF (JOINT) – A process for connecting the ends of two wood members by fashioning an overlapping joint so that the material forms a continuous piece of the same cross section. An "edge scarf" is made by cutting across the longer side of the plank. A "flat-scarf" is a similar process, cutting across the shorter side of the piece. The joint may be secured with an adhesive and/or wood screws, or through-bolted with threaded rods or drifts, with or without clench rings. (as in "a scarfed joint") A "straight scarf" is made simply by tapering and overlapping the two pieces. A "notched (nibbed) scarf" is similar except the ends of this scarf are nibbed into a notch to enhance the integrity of the joint. A "hooked scarf," preferred in joining keel, keelson and other longitudinal members is interrupted by a Z-like deviation at mid-scarf, forming a hook which greatly resists tensile stress. *Martha's* boom was rebuilt with a "clothespin scarf" or "V-scarf," consisting of one end cut to the shape of a long wedge, fitting into a corresponding cutting away in the other piece. Metal banding is common for this type of scarf if care is taken to eliminate protrusions that would snag or damage a line or sail.

SHEER PLANK – The upper-most side plank, just under the covering board, fastened to the head of the frames at the deck edge.

SHEER POLE – A wooden batten seized across two or more mast shrouds, above the deadeyes or turnbuckles, through which holes are drilled for belaying pins.

SHEET – A line used to control the foot of the sail to gain the best advantage of the wind. The sheet may be connected to the clew of the sail, a club or a boom.

SHROUD – Part of the standing rigging. Wire cable, fitted in pairs, looped around each side of the mast at the hounds, extending down to the deck edge, connected to *chain plates* by means of a turnbuckle arrangement to support the mast laterally.

SPECTACLE IRON – A device forged from a small steel rod, which slightly resembles spectacles used to improve eyesight. There is a center loop through which the head stay is passed when setting up the standing rig, on either side of which there are smaller loops to which the port and starboard *lazy-jacks* of the *jib sail* are attached.

STAVING – Where the bottom hull planking, in herring bone pattern, steadily rises to a more obtuse angle from the keel rabbet and makes a transition to a thwartship pattern, becoming vertical at the stem rabbet. These planks are more complex to fashion because of the varying angle between the keel and chine. Traditionally, the pieces are selected from thicker stock and roughly shaped, for the inner surface to bear solidly on keel and chine log. The planks are then fastened to the boat and faired (fayed) to the desired surface.

STEERING GEAR ASSEMBLY – An arrangement of gears by which the rudder is turned to control the direction of the vessel. The apparatus, called a push-pull mechanism, consists of a left-handed and right-handed shaft, connected to opposite sides of a cross-head tiller, which is connected to the head of the rudder post. The apparatus is powered by the ship's wheel, which is of sufficient size and mechanical advantage for one person to control. The gear assembly is covered with a lidded box with an opening for the wheel shaft.

STEM PIECE – A vertical member, part of the bow structure, that rest on the forward end of the *keel timber*, raking forward at a slight angle. It is trapezoidal in cross section tapered forward. Its after edge is rabbeted to provide the fastening surface for the first bottom strake and all the side planks.

STERN POST – Usually a central timber at the stern, based on the keel. On *Martha Lewis, actually two transom frames on each side of the rudder post,* which provide support for the upper and lower transom beams.

STRINGER – A fore-and-aft plank fastened to the inboard surface of the bottom planking; two are required on each side, spaced equally between keel and chine.

STRONGBACK – A combination of several timbers and knees installed athwartships at a designated point near midship to reinforce the hull below the dredge rollers.

TONNAGE – An admeasured calculation of carrying capacity. Gross tonnage relates roughly to the cargo carrying capacity above and below decks, while the net tonnage is gross tonnage minus the non-lading space.

TOPPING LIFT – A *halyard* leading from the outer end of the boom to a block at the masthead, thence to the deck, the purpose of which is lifting (topping) the boom.

TOPSIDE – That portion of a vessel's hull surface above the load-waterline. Also, on or above the weather deck.

TRAILBOARD – An ornamental plank on either side of the longhead (or cutwater), with a small end piece continuing onto the stem. When the boat's name is included it may be called a "name board." On *Martha Lewis* there is also a separate unadorned name board on either side of the bulwarks forward of the shroud chain plates. Her name and home port are also painted on the transom.

TRANSOM BEAMS – The <u>upper transom beam</u> is actually the last deck beam at the after end of the boat, situated forward of the *"stern post"* and intermediate transom frames, bracketed at each end by the *plank sheer (covering board)*. Quarter knews are let into the ends of these beams to create a flush surface for covering boards and margin piece. The *lower transom beam* is actually a pair of port and starboard half-beams, joining the chine logs and the rudder post assembly.

TRAVELER – A ring, thimble or strap which travels along a horse.

TRUNK CABIN – A cabin that extends only partially above the deck. On *Martha*, the below deck portion is fitted with three berths. At the aft end of the cabin top is a companionway consisting of an opening with a sliding hatch, commonly known as a "dog house" allowing easy access to the cabin below deck.

WHISKER STAY – A chain, smaller than the bowsprit guy which serves as an outrigger running horizontally from the outer end of the bowsprit to an eyebolt in the top rail of the bulwark several feet forward of the shroud *chain plates*, and a few feet aft of the stem.

WINDERS – An arrangement mounted approximately midship, consisting of an engine, gear-box and a port and a starboard windlass specifically designed for hauling in or letting out cables attached to oyster dredges.

~ *Appendix B* ~

DREDGE BOATS OF THE CHESAPEAKE BAY

Allen Rawl and I traveled over much of the Eastern Shore of Maryland in the fall of 1993 to locate and identify all known extant dredge boats on the Bay. Most of those found floating were at docks in marinas, primarily at Deal and Tilghman Islands. Many others were found blocked-up in fields or on marina grounds, and several were seen sinking in the mud in marshes and small creeks.

In 1983-84 the Maryland Historical Trust (MHT) prepared a Maryland Historic Sites Inventory of all existing skipjacks for nomination in the National Register of Historic Places. Many, but not all, were given Register status in 1985. Those of more recent construction were not ac-

Fred Hecklinger and Allen Rawl after the Cambridge Skipjack Race.
September, 1999.

cepted. This survey gave each boat a number prefixed by a letter denoting the county in which it resided, e.g., T for Talbot, D for Dorchester, S for Somerset. It provided significant detail about each vessel's origins, owners, construction features, rigging, and size. The findings are referenced briefly here. For reference on-line, search National Register of Historic Places Inventory – NPS Focus– Skipjack Fleet.

Not suprisingly, our research showed that skipjack measurements are notoriously difficult to confirm. They originate from various sources and are ambigious as to definition and standards used.

An especially in-depth survey was performed in 1988 by Fred Hecklinger, a marine surveyor from Annapolis with decades of personal experience with these Bay craft. The study was made for the Maryland Historical Trust as part of a Skipjack Preservation Plan. This study is really quite extensive and detailed. The primary emphasis was on each boat's condition, but Fred added his own historical notes and recommendations about preservation. His findings are only briefly included here.

Fred was a valued expert advisor during the reconstruction of *Martha Lewis*, and was sailing master on many of her skipjack races.

The list that follows represents all the dredge boats that we could identify in 1993. Where possible, I have recorded their conditions at various stages, quoting individuals who knew them directly. This accounting can do but poor justice to the rich and complex histories attendant to each boat and to the legions of watermen and their families who depended on them for a living. This list was updated to 2015 (see italics) from word-of-mouth accounts and from scattered internet sources. Omissions and errors are, with apology, my own.

====================

– Ada Fears –

BUILDER:	YEAR:	SITE:
Curtis Applegarth	1968	Oxford, MD

She was sold to New Jersey, and then returned to Chesapeake Bay. In the 1970s she was called *Lady Agnes* and was a dredge boat. *Ada Fears* was sailed in 2009 Deal Island Race. She is the smallest remaining skipjack. In 2015 she was available for sale at Scott's Cove Marina, Chance, Maryland by owner Brian Conrad.

- *Ada Mae* -

BUILDER:	YEAR:	SITE:
Capt. Ralph Hodges	1915	Rose Bay, NC

LENGTH:	BEAM WIDTH:	DEPTH:	NET REG. WT.:
32.6'	12.0'	2.3'	8 Tons

In 2015 she was at Carolina Coastal Classrooms, New Bern, North Carolina. *Ada Mae* is the only remaining North Carolina skipjack. A long aftercabin was added at some time.

- *Amy Mister* -

BUILDER:	YEAR:	SITE:
---	1914	Oriole, MD

LENGTH:	BEAM WIDTH:	DEPTH:	NET REG. WT.:
57.0'	19.7'	5.6'	25 Tons

Bay Dredging License #46. Not included in the 1983 inventory, nor in the National Historical Registry. The 1988 survey found her dead since approximately 1977 at Whitehaven, Maryland on the Wicomico River. Local waterman, Charles Abbott, Jr. reported that she had had the same owner as *Ralph T. Webster*, probably Capt. William Berridge. In 1993 we found her in a severely decayed state on the shoreline at Whitehaven.

Amy Mister. Whitehaven, MD on the Wicomico River. October 1993.

- *Anna McGarvey* -

BUILDER:	YEAR:	SITE:
Melbourne Smith	1980-1981	---

LENGTH:	BEAM WIDTH:	DEPTH:	NET REG. WT.:
45.3'	15.7'	---	8 Tons

INCLUDED IN:
• MHT Inventory 1983: T-526 • 1988 Survey • 1993 Search

The first owner was Mike Ashford who owned McGarvey's Saloon in Annapolis, Maryland. Fred Hecklinger's 1988 survey related that she was "built in
1980-81 by Melbourne Smith, builder of the *Pride of Baltimore*, at the same time as
the rebuild of *Minnie V.* She was sailed by at least two captains until she was presented to the Maryland Department of Natural Resources, which did not keep
her up. "She was a superior sailer when handled well." Fred said he cut her trail
boards. In 1988, he found her with considerable rot at the D.N.R. station at Deal
Island. In 1993 we found her severely deteriorated, but floating with the help of
pumps, at the Crisfield, Maryland Maritime Museum. She was later said to be
on shore at Kent Island, Maryland. In 2015 she was being restored by Joe Laber
at Cambridge, Maryland.

Anna McGarvey. Crisfield, MD. July 1993.

– *Bernice J.* –

BUILDER:	YEAR:	SITE:
William Thomas Young	1904	Young's Creek, VA

LENGTH:	BEAM WIDTH:	DEPTH:	NET REG. WT.:
40.6'	14.5'	3.3'	8 Tons

INCLUDED IN:
• MHT Inventory 1983: T-526 • MHT Inventory 1985: K-539
• 1985 National Register p 69, #885 ref: 85001946 • 1988 Survey • 1993 Search

Dan Dize recalled that "Coonie Evans of Ewell owned her for years. Cap'n Will Smith had 'er for many years. He was a right good dredger an' e' made some money into 'er." She was also owned by Mervin or Melvin Christy of Crisfield, the first black waterman to own a skipjack. She sailed out of Chestertown. In 1981 she was purchased by the Echo Hill Outdoor School, near Worton, Maryland, in Kent County, by Capt. Andrew McCowan. Fred Hecklinger found her in "bad shape" during the 1988 Maryland Historical Trust Survey, at the Echo Hill School. We located her there on land in 1993, in very decayed condition and seemingly abandoned. *She was broken up in 1999.*

Bernice J. Near Worton, MD. Summer 1994.

– Caleb W. Jones –

BUILDER:	YEAR:	SITE:
C. H. Rice	1953	Reedville, VA

LENGTH:	BEAM WIDTH:	DEPTH:	NET REG. WT.:
44.1'	15.5' or 16.5'	2.5'	8 Tons

INCLUDED IN:
• MHT Inventory 1983: S-230 • 1988 Survey • 1993 Search

C. H. Rice also built the *City of Crisfield*. In 1985 she was owned by Dickie Webster of Wenona, Somerset County. She was generally in good condition and was working. She had apparently sunk outside Baltimore, and had been repaired. In the 1988 survey Fred Hecklinger reported that she was still owned by Richard (Dickie) Webster at Wenona and was maintained well. He described her as "not a prime sailer," but said that Dickie Webster was one of the leaders of the Deal Island fleet. Deck beams and decking had been replaced in 1987, and there was "serious rot in the stem below decks and in the strongback aft of the mast." In 1993 we found her still owned by Richard Webster. She sailed in the Deal Island Race on 9/6/93. She had had repairs at the Living Classroom in Baltimore in 1992. We noted that the bow sprit was not joined to the Samson post and dredge rollers were in rough condition, but that she was still capable of dredging. *She continued working thereafter, and was in the Deal Island Race in 2015.*

– City of Crisfield –

BUILDER:	YEAR:	SITE:
C. H. Rice	1948-1949	Reedville, VA

LENGTH:	BEAM WIDTH:	DEPTH:	NET REG. WT.:
44.7'	15.8'	3.7'	10 Tons

INCLUDED IN:
• MHT Inventory 1983: S-231 • 1988 Survey • 1993 Search

Bay Dredging License #1491. In the 1988 Maryland Historical Trust survey her owner was Arthur Daniels, Jr., in Wenona, Somerset County. She was in poor condition with extensive rot. In 1993 she was still owned by Arthur Daniels, also the owner of a crab shed in Wenona. She was in fair condition only, superficially weak, but sailed in the Deal Island Race 9/6/93. *She underwent restoration at the Chesapeake Bay Maritime Museum thereafter, and participated in the 2015 Deal Island race; her captain was Art Daniels.*

Caleb W. Jones. Wenona, Deal Island. November 1998.

City of Crisfield. Wenona, Deal Island. June 1993. Courtesy Allen Rawl.

– *City of Norfolk* –

BUILDER:	YEAR:	SITE:
G. W. Horseman	c. 1900	Deal Island, MD

LENGTH:	BEAM WIDTH:	DEPTH:	NET REG. WT.:
45.5'	15.2'	3.5'	9 Tons

INCLUDED IN:
• 1988 Survey • 1993 Search

A sister ship to the *E. C. Collier*, she was owned by the Allegheny Beverage Corporation from Baltimore, which renamed her *Allegheny* and restored her in the 1960s. They donated her in 1978 to the City of Norfolk, Virginia, who again changed her name. Fred Hecklinger said that he fashioned her mast in 1977 and that she had been converted into a yacht. She appeared in the Deal Island race on 9/6/93 and superficially seemed in good repair. She motored out and sails were raised, but she did not race. I*n approximately 2005 the City of Norfolk gave her to a non-profit organization in Cape Charles, Virginia. In 2015 she was at Deal Island.*

City of Norfolk (*George W. Collier*). Deal Island Race. September 1993.
Courtesy Allen Rawl.

– *Clarence Crockett* –

BUILDER:	YEAR:	SITE:
---	1908	Deep Creek, VA (Accomac)

LENGTH:	BEAM WIDTH:	DEPTH:	NET REG. WT.:
44.6'	14.7'	3.0'	7 Tons

INCLUDED IN:
• MHT Inventory 1983: S-232 • 1985 National Register p 67, #853 ref: 8500079
• 1988 Survey • 1993 Search

Bay Dredging License #48. At the time of the MHT Inventory, the owner was Lowdie Horner of Wenona, Deal Island. In 1988 Fred Hecklinger found her being rebuilt at Crockett's Boatyard in Crisfield, Maryland. His survey report relates that "she sank in March 1988 due to multiple short planks, striking a mark in Tangier Sound. She was taken to Crisfield in bad shape." There was "extensive rot in the keel, chine, side and bottom planking, deck beams and mast." He felt she would not work soon, and would "most likely be put aside." In 1993 I found her at Deal Island, owned by Paul Holland. She appeared to be sinking at the dock, with a kink in the rail and a bent boom and nearly dead. Nonetheless, she sailed in the Deal Island race on 9/6/93. *She was said to be cut up in 2010 at Wenona.*

Clarence Crockett. Wenona, Deal Island. June 1993. Courtesy Allen Rawl.

– *Claude W. Somers* –

BUILDER:	YEAR:	SITE:
W. Thomas Young	1911	Young Creek, VA (Accomac)

LENGTH:	BEAM WIDTH:	DEPTH:	REG. WT.:
42.5'	14.3'	3.0'	Net: 6 Tons Gross: 8 Tons

INCLUDED IN:
• MHT Inventory 1983: T-527 • 1985 National Register p 67, #859 ref: 85001085
• 1988 Survey • 1993 Search

She was commissioned by Thomas Edward Somers of Crisfield, Maryland. In the 1988 Maryland Historical Trust Survey, Fred Hecklinger related that she had been under several owners, and was a fast sailer. She sank on 3/4/1977 in a 70-knot squall near Hooper's Strait Lighthouse, in one of the worst fishing disasters in Bay history. Six crewmen drowned, including Captain Thompson Wallace of Chance, Maryland. Dave Faulkner told me the story: "*Claude W. Somers* capsized one day in Hooper Straits. I talked to Cap'n Orville Parks about it and he told me an all-black crew, family mostly, all drowned when she turned over. Cap'n Orville said he was there that day on the *Joy Parks*, when the weather hit. He pulled the sails in, got 'em tied down, turned tail-to and let her scud. All he could see for about an hour was rainbows. It blew so hard, it blew the fog off, and the rainbows were everywhere. When things settled down, he had scudded up to Cambridge. Some of the others capsized and others probably piled up on the shore."

Claude W. Somers was owned thereafter by D. K. Bond of Crownsville, Maryland and by Darryl Larrimore of Tilghman Island. She worked until 1983 when she was bought by Alfred Gary Lambert and underwent a 17-year restoration. In 1988 she was being rebuilt slowly. In 1993 I found her at a marina on Chicken Point Road, Tilghman Island up on blocks, with a nearly new bottom and a good, recent deck. Bob Lambert was approximately 70 years old and was slowly restoring her. *At his death in 1999 Lambert's children gave her to the Reedville Fisherman's Museum in Reedville, Northumberland County, Virginia. Restoration was undertaken at Cockrell's marine railway in 2000-01. She resided at the Museum in 2015.*

Claude W. Somers. Tilghman Island, MD. November 1993.

– Connie Frances –

BUILDER:	YEAR:	SITE:
Francis Goddard	1984-1985	St. Mary's County, MD

LENGTH:	BEAM WIDTH:	DEPTH:	NET REG. WT.:
56.0'	21.0'	4.3'	---

INCLUDED IN:
• 1988 Survey

Francis Goddard also built the *Dee of St. Mary's*. In 1988 Fred Hecklinger deemed her "large and bulky," not a good sailer, but ready to "work this season." We did not visit her in 1993. Goddard was said to have her for sale that year.

======================

– Dee of St. Mary's –

		SITE:
BUILDER:	YEAR:	Piney Point or St.
Francis Goddard	1979	George's Island, MD
		(St. Mary's County)

LENGTH:	BEAM WIDTH:	DEPTH:	NET REG. WT.:
56.0' or 55.0'	19.5' or 18.5'	6.0' or 3.9'	25 Tons

INCLUDED IN:
• MHT Inventory 1983: SM-366 • 1988 Survey

She was designed by William Hall of Solomon's Island, St. Mary's County. Bay Dredging License #16. She was the second largest skipjack ever built. In 1988 she was owned by Jackie Russell. Fred Hecklinger recorded that she had been well maintained since construction and sailed remarkably well. She occasionally was used for sailing parties. We did not visit her in 1993. *Capt. Jack Russell still owned her in 2007. In 2015 she was at St. George's Island south of St. Mary's City, Maryland.*

– E. C. Collier –

BUILDER:	YEAR:	SITE:
G. W. Horseman	1910	Deal Island, MD

LENGTH:	BEAM WIDTH:	DEPTH:	REG. WT.:
52.0'	17.9'	4.5' or 4.3'	Gross: 19 Tons Net: 14 Tons

INCLUDED IN:
• MHT Inventory 1983: T-528 • 1985 National Register ref: 85001087
• 1988 Survey • 1993 Search

The 1988 survey recorded her as having been operated for 20 years by John Larrimore of Tilghman Island, who died in 1983. She was worked thereafter by Larrimore's nephew, but had "not worked in the past three years." Fred Hecklinger recalled her as a good dredge boat, but a slow sailer in races. In 1993 Calvert Parks recalled that "it would drown you to dredge it, because to pull a dredge you'd need a 20-mile breeze. I helped plumb the mast, and she worked better." That same year we found her nearly dead at the Chesapeake Bay Maritime Museum, to be painted and used as a display. *In 2015 she was on display under cover at the Museum in St. Michaels, Maryland.*

E. C. Collier. Chesapeake Bay Maritime Museum,
St. Michaels, MD. September 1993.

– Edna Lockwood –

BUILDER:	YEAR:	SITE:
John B. Harrison	1889	---

LENGTH:	BEAM WIDTH:	DEPTH:	NET REG. WT.:
53.3'	15.23'	2.6'	---

INCLUDED IN:

• 1985 National Register ref: 86000258 • 1988 Survey

Harrison's bugeye was a 9-log canoe with 7 owners between 1899 and 1967. After that, she was converted to a yacht. The Chesapeake Maritime Museum restored her in 1975-79 to her 1910 appearance. In the 1988 Maryland Historical Trust survey, Fred Hecklinger noted that "she sailed well if properly handled. Extensively rebuilt at St. Michael's museum." *She became a National Historic Landmark on 4/19/94 and sailed in the Chesapeake Appreciation Days Race in October, 1994.*

====================================

– Elsworth –

BUILDER:	YEAR:	SITE:
Mitchell Hubbard or Robert H. Thomas	1901	Hudson, MD (Dorchester)

LENGTH:	BEAM WIDTH:	DEPTH:	NET REG. WT.:
39.9'	14.3'	3.1'	8 Tons

INCLUDED IN:

• MHT Inventory 1983: T-529 • 1985 National Register #862 ref: 85001088
• 1988 Survey

She was commissioned by Hilary Wingate and named for his son Joseph Elsworth Wingate. Bay Dredging License #22. Osylee Lewis said, "she was owned by my brother Norris before he retired. She was difficult to handle. They called her the 'Hellsworth.'" Norris first worked as a hand on *Elsworth*, then bought her one day after Hurricane Hazel in 1954, from Irving F. Cannon, according to Norris' daughter, Dot Shortall. At the time of the Maryland Historical Trust Survey, she recently had been sold to the District of Columbia which planned to restore her and lease her to a Tilghman Island captain. The 1988 survey stated that she was skippered after 1978 by Darryl Larrimore, the youngest captain in the oyster fleet. Next she was owned and worked by Robbie Doyle of Tilghman Island and was brought to an excellent condition. After 1988 she was on the Chester River, and was owned by the Echo Hill School. *She entered the Chesapeake Appreciation Days Race in October, 1994. A rebuild was begun in 1996. In 2015 she was docked at Chestertown Maryland.*

Edna Lockwood. Bugeye. Chesapeake Bay Maritime Museum.
St. Michaels, MD. September 1993.

Elsworth. October 1993.

- *Esther F.* -

Builder:	Year:	Site:
---	1954	Fairmount, MD

Length:	Beam Width:	Depth:	Reg. Wt.:
39.5'	13.3'	3.8'	Gross: 10 Tons

Included In:
• MHT Inventory 1983: T-530 • 1988 Survey • 1993 Search

Bay Dredging License #2. She was not accepted in the National Register due to her age. The 1988 Maryland Historical Trust survey related that she was owned by Fred H. and Wendell Bradley until Wendell was killed in an auto accident in 1967. Then she was sold to Connecticut as a yacht from 1967-1977. Fred Hecklinger recorded that she was then "bought by Bart Murphy in approximately 1980, was reworked to good standards, and was active since. She was a top sailer and was fitted for two masts." She was finally given to the Chesapeake Bay Maritime Museum which then sold her to Buck Garvin of Tilghman Island, who then returned her to oystering. In 1988 she had a full cabin, was in "good shape," and participated in the Deal Island Race. In 1992 she was owned by Bart Murphy and was working. On 9/20/1993 we found her at Tilghman in bad shape, with much surface rot, and full of water.

- *Ethel Lewis* -

Builder:	Year:	Site:
---	1906	Chesconnessex, VA

Length:	Beam Width:	Depth:	Net Reg. Wt.:
45'	14'	---	---

Included In:

After working as a dredge boat for decades, she was sold to an Islip, N.Y. private owner, who converted her to a yacht. She was abandoned at Brooklyn Naval Yard. Donors arranged for her transport to Onancock, VA, where she remained on shore in 2005-2009, and for lack of funds, was burned in 2010.

Esther F. Tilghman Island, MD. September 1993.

– *Fannie L. Daughtery* –

BUILDER:	YEAR:	SITE:
Jim Daughtery	1904	Crisfield, MD

LENGTH:	BEAM WIDTH:	DEPTH:	NET REG. WT.:
41.3'	15.3'	3.6'	8 Tons

INCLUDED IN:
• MHT Inventory 1983: S-233 • 1985 National Register p 67, #885 ref: 85001081
• 1988 Survey • 1993 Search

Bay Dredging License #58. Her lines were used in 1955 to build the *H. M. Krentz* in Harryhogan, Virginia. Dan Dize recalled, "the *Daugherty* was the first dredge boat that I owned, and I had her 30 years. I put a mast in her." Dave Faulkner related, "Did you hear the bad stories about her? What I was told was that she drowned two crews. The last one was in about 1939. The wind hit these guys in a heavy fog. They were laying at their dredges when the wind hit them out of the northwest, and she capsized." She was owned by Capt. Norman Benton when entered on the National Register on 5/11/1985. In the 1988 Survey Norman Benton was the owner and captain. She was in relatively good condition, "despite neglect," and was not actively dredging. There was considerable rot. Norman then sold her to his son, Delmas Benton. When seen on 7/19/1993 she was alongside the road in Wenona, Deal Island, Maryland. She was slightly hogged [sagging fore and aft], the decking was laid in sections, the mast was wedged far forward and the boom was banded and split. She was not yet dead, and Delmas Benton was still working her. *She sailed in the Deal Island Race on 9/6/93, Chesapeake Appreciation Days Race in October, 1993, and was still working when she sailed in the Deal Island Race in 2015 under Captain Delmas Benton.*

Fannie L. Daugherty.
Deal Island Race.
September 1993.
Courtesy of
Allen Rawl.

- *F. C. Lewis, Jr.* -

BUILDER:	YEAR:	SITE:
---	1907	Hopkins or Hunting Creek, VA (Accomac)

LENGTH:	BEAM WIDTH:	DEPTH:	NET REG. WT.:
39.0'	14.6'	3.0'	6 Tons

INCLUDED IN:
• MHT Inventory 1983: S-234 • 1985 National Register p 67, #854 ref: 85001080
• 1988 Survey • 1993 Search

When she was entered in the National Register of Historic Places, she was owned by Stanford White of Wenona, Deal Island, Maryland. She was still owned by Stanford White in the 1988 Survey, but as Fred Hecklinger recorded, "had not been rigged to dredge in about 8 years. She was a great light air boat." She had previously raced, but was now sailed only occasionally. In 1993 she was still owned by Stanford White at Wenona. She had been fiberglased, appeared in rough condition when seen at the dock, with potted flowers on deck. *In 2015 her address was Denton, Maryland, far up the Choptank River, and she was reportedly blocked up on land.*

F. C. Lewis. Wenona, Deal Island, MD. October 1993.

- *Flora A. Price* -

BUILDER:	YEAR:	SITE:
---	---	---

LENGTH:	BEAM WIDTH:	DEPTH:	NET REG. WT.:
---	---	---	---

INCLUDED IN:

Built at Chance, Maryland in 1910, she dredged for many years, and then was used by Sea Scouts in Wilmington, Delaware. She later resided at Denton, Maryland at the Harford Town Maritime Center. Upkeep was prohibitive and the James B. Richardson Museum in Cambridge took her over in 2005. She rotted and sank at the dock, was taken out in pieces, and was burned in 2013.

═══════════════════════════════

- *Geneva May* -

BUILDER:	YEAR:	SITE:
---	1908	Wenona, MD

LENGTH:	BEAM WIDTH:	DEPTH:	REG. WT.:
49.8'	16.6'	2.2'	Gross: 15 Tons Net: 11 Tons

INCLUDED IN:

She was not listed in either the Inventory or the Register. Her crew including Capt. Bill Hubbard, survived the February 3, 1939 storm in which 9 watermen died. Dave Faulkner recalled that Darryl Larrimore bought her in North Carolina for $1 and brought her to Tilghman Island at the foot of Fairland Road. She had too much rot to repair. "He ran her up in the mud, (in 1979) then was required to move her to another creek, where she sank again. She could be reached by a path on Bay Neck Road." *In October 1993 we located her at Tilghman in shallow water, completely dead.*

Geneva May. Tilghman Island, MD. October 1993.

- *Helen Virginia* -

BUILDER: Gus Forbush	YEAR: 1948 or 1949	SITE: Crisfield, MD

LENGTH: 43.2'	BEAM WIDTH: 15.6'	DEPTH: 2.2'	NET REG. WT.: 10.25 Tons

INCLUDED IN:
• MHT Inventory 1983: S-235 • 1988 Survey • 1993 Search

Bay Dredging License #53. She was not entered on the National Register due to her age. Osylee Lewis recalled that Richard Hubbard used to own her, then "Eugene Rippens (sp?) bought her, over t' Hoopersville." Dan Dize remembered, "I know that thing sails. She's the onliest dern boat that come up on me wid a leadin' breeze at Sandy Point." In the 1988 Survey she was owned by Capt. Jack Parkinson of Chance, Maryland, who worked her since 1977. "She could be a fast sailer," per Fred Hecklinger. Parkinson sold her to Ernie Barlow in Dorchester County in the 1990s, then Barlow sold her to Robert Wilson. When seen on 7/19/1993 she was hogged and rotting at Rock Creek, Chance, Deal Island. *She was in the Deal Island races in at least 9/93 and 2006. In 2007 she sailed out of Cambridge, Maryland. In 2013 Wilson sold her to Capt. 'Stoney Whitelock, who planned to restore her along with* Kathryn *at Scott's Cove Marina, Chance, Maryland. She won the Deal Island Race of 9/1/14, sailed by the first all-female skipjack crew. In 2015 she taking out passengers for sailing trips, Capt. Katarina Ennerfelt.*

Helen Virginia. **Rock Creek, Chance, MD. July 1993. Courtesy Allen Rawl.**

- *Hilda M. Willing* -

BUILDER:	YEAR:	SITE:
---	1905	Oriole, MD

LENGTH:	BEAM WIDTH:	DEPTH:	REG. WT.:
40.0'	14.0'	3.1'	Gross: 8 Tons Net: 6 Tons

INCLUDED IN:
• MHT Inventory 1983: T-531 • 1985 National Register ref: 85001089
• 1988 Survey • 1993 Search

Dave Faulkner told us that "Pete Sweitzer came out of service about '45 and dredged with another guy, Hardy Jackson before he bought the *Willin'*. She was a gem. He took good care of her. We used to be good buddies, that is, until one day, for some reason, he got angry with a few of us. He hit some oysters on a place called Diamonds, and we all went down, which we usually did. When we got there I heard a damn shotgun. Bam! And a buoy sank. Pete had shot Hardy Jackson's buoy. Hardy sailed away. And then he shot again and cut Wadey Murphy close. Anyway, they all sailed away, one by one. Then Pete shot again, hitting the water near where I was at the wheel. The next time he shot, he hit my sails, and the BB's rolled down on my crew. So my brother-in-law ran down to the cabin and got our shotgun. Every time Pete would shoot, we would shoot. We stayed there until we all ran out of shells. We were far enough away from each other that no damage was done. Since then Pete and I have patched everything up, but I hardly see him anymore."

At the time of the Skipjack Preservation Plan Survey by the Maryland Historical Trust in 1988, Robert "Pete" Sweitzer of Tilghman Island, had been her owner and operator for 41 years. She was "well maintained, does not race." In 1993 she was found at Tilghman Island in the best shape of all the skipjacks we surveyed. *She became a National Historic Landmark on 4/19/94. She dredged in at least the 2005-06 season and was berthed at Tilghman in 2015.*

Hilda M. Willing.
Dogwood Marina,
Tilghman Island, MD.
July 1993.
Courtesy Allen Rawl.

- *H. M. Krentz* -

			SITE:
BUILDER:	**YEAR:**		Harryhogan, VA
Herman Krentz	1955		(Northumberland)
			Yeocomico River

			REG. WT.:
LENGTH:	**BEAM WIDTH:**	**DEPTH:**	Gross: 9 Tons
44.3'	15.6'	4.9'	Net: 8 Tons

INCLUDED IN:

• MHT Inventory 1983: S-236 • 1985 National Register ref: 85001089
• 1988 Survey • 1993 Search

Bay Dredging License #59. Dan Dize recalled that Herman Krentz took *Fannie L. Daugherty's* measurements to build *H.M. Krentz* "'cause he told me he did. He was a real good carpenter, but he built *H. M. Krentz* a little too narra. He should have built her a little bit fuller. They say she would wall out, you know, c'reen out .. like yer gonna capsize all the time." At the time of the 1988 Skipjack Preservation Survey her owners were Edward Theodore 'Ted' Webster and Mrs. Clifton Webster, Wenona, Deal Island, Maryland. According to the survey: "idle last year. In remarkably good condition. Some rot in deck, deck house, wheelbox, bowsprit. Won at Sandy Point and Deal Island Races on several occasions." In 1993 the owner was Ed Farley. She had a new mast, was cruising, not rigged for oystering. Sailed in the Deal Island Race 9/6/1993. *She raced in at least the 2007 Deal Island Race, the Choptank Heritage Skipjack Race, and took passengers out of St. Michaels, Maryland as late as 2015.*

H. M. Krentz. Deal Island Race. September 6, 1993.

- *Howard* -

BUILDER:	YEAR:	SITE:
---	1909	Deep Creek, VA (South of Parksley)

LENGTH:	BEAM WIDTH:	DEPTH:	NET REG. WT.:
45.0'	15.3'	3.1'	8 Tons

INCLUDED IN:
• MHT Inventory 1983: S-237 • 1985 National Register ref: 85001089
• 1988 Survey • 1993 Search

Before the 1983-84 survey, she had been owned by Jack Parks of Rock Creek, Maryland, and had a complete rebuild at the Living Classroom at Baltimore. In 1988 her owner was Stanley Daniels of Wenona, Deal Island, Maryland, and her condition was poor, with rot about the deck, in need of a "complete rebuild." In 1993 Osylee Lewis related that she "sank a year or two ago in Cambridge harbor. Stan Daniels owned her, Art Daniels' boy." Dave Faulkner recalled, "I can tell you a story about the *Howard*. We were taking up spat for the State, seed orsters on Parson's Island up on Eastern Bay, and we were carryin' 'em off to diff'rent places, West River, Chester River. The *Howard* was up there and myself, the only two boats. We were circlin', shoveling the shells, and a damn seal came up, played with us, clappin' his hands. He played with us a half hour. We were 6 men on my boat, besides me, and the *Howard* had 4 or 5 men. We couldn'a all been drunk, but that's what they accused us of. I never heard of such a thing, in this water, but it really happened." Howard *was sailed in the 9/6/93 Deal Island Race by Capt. Arthur Stanley Daniels, Jr. In 2015 she was docked at Wenona, Deal Island.*

Howard. **Baltimore, MD at Living Classroom. July 1993.
Courtesy Allen Rawl.**

- Ida May -

BUILDER:	YEAR:	SITE:
---	1906	Deep Creek, VA (Accomac)

LENGTH:	BEAM WIDTH:	DEPTH:	REG. WT.:
42.2'	14.4'	3.3'	Gross: 10 Tons / Net: 7 Tons

INCLUDED IN:

• MHT Inventory 1983: S-238 • 1985 National Register p 67 #851 ref: #85001077
• 1988 Survey • 1993 Search

Oyster dredge number 41. She was bought by Melvin Beauchamp and Melvin Bevins in the 1950s, and rebuilt in 1954 at the Krentz Boatyard in Harryhogan, Virginia, or in 1955 at Reedville, Virginia. Osylee Lewis said, "She used to be Orville's (Parks) first dredge boat. He came out of service and his father gave it to him." Dan Dize remembered *Ida May*: "We were caught in a gale, and my brother was in *Annie Lee*, an' I was in the *Doraty* (*Daugherty*), an' 'ere was this *Ida May*. We were up on Bloody Point, just above the lighthouse, dredgin' orsters, an' the weather report said it's agoin'a be a heavy wind. We scudded down there, an' we thought *Ida May* was gonna get lost shor'in the devil. He let hisself get way too leeward, an' had ta get back up. We all got down to the lower end of Poplar Island, an' we had not a damn prig of sail on her, neither bit. We scudded into Tilghman just the same as a steamboat." Dave Faulkner recalled that "years ago, say in the '40s, Cap'n Johnnie Capsack, down in Fairbank at the lower part of Tilghman Island, owned the *Ida May*. During the Hazel storm of 1954, the eye of the hurricane came right over Deal Island. We had winds over a hundred mile an hour, and the *Ida May* ended up on the highway." In 1968 she was bought by Elbert W. Gladden, of Chance, Maryland, from Melvin 'Fish' Bevins. (Elbert had also owned *Somerset* and *Mamie Mister*).

Gladden was her owner at the time of the MHT Inventory in 1985. The 1988 Survey noted substantial rot around the deck and hatches, many short planks on deck, and a need for a complete rebuild. Elbert Gladden was still her owner. In 1993 we found her much improved. She had been significantly rebuilt above the waterline. She was owned by A. W. Hall Insurance, Salisbury, and Capt. Gordon Gladden sailed her in the Deal Island Race on 9/6/1993. *She became a National Historic Landmark on 4/19/94, and raced at her home base of Deal Island in 2005. She capsized during the Cambridge Race in 2013.*

Ida May. Skipjack. Deal Island, MD. June 1993. Courtesy Allen Rawl.

- *Joy Parks* -

BUILDER:	YEAR:	SITE:
William Thomas Young	1936	(near) Parksley, VA

LENGTH:	BEAM WIDTH:	DEPTH:	NET REG. WT.:
46.4'	15.5'	4.0'	---

INCLUDED IN:

Commissioned and owned by Capt. Robert W. W. Parks and then by his son, Orville. Orville and his crew survived the February 3, 1939 storm in which 9 watermen died. Young also built *Bernice J.* and *Claude W. Somers. She was moved to Washington, D. C. at the Smithsonian in 2004, and then to the Piney Point Lighthouse Museum, on the Potomac River in St. Mary's County, Maryland, in 2007. In 2015 she was on permanent display inside the Museum.*

- Kathryn -

BUILDER:	YEAR:	SITE:
E. J. Daughtery	1901	Crisfield, MD

LENGTH:	BEAM WIDTH:	DEPTH:	NET REG. WT.:
50.0'	16.8'	4.2'	12 Tons

INCLUDED IN:

• MHT Inventory 1983: T-532 • 1985 National Register p 68, #864 ref: 85001090, 1994 National Historical Landmark • 1988 Survey • 1993 Search

Bay Dredging License #21. *Kathryn* underwent a complete rebuild in Virginia in 1954. Malcolm Wheatley held an interest in her in 1945 and owned her outright in 1963. Osylee Lewis said she was "owned by my brother-in-law Malcolm Wheatley, my sister Edna's husband. She won some races at Deal Island. Boy, that was a work boat. First thing you can recognize her by is that copper ball on top, the only one I know with a copper ball. An' she's got a high bowsplit (sic)." Dave Faulkner recalled that Malcolm Wheatley had her rebuilt, bottom, sides, and deck, and that the work was "finished on Labor Day, 1970, when she was 69 years old."

In 1975 she was bought by Johnnie R. Parkinson, Jr. and was moved to Crisfield. In 1981 Herman Russell Dize owned her with William James Roe, Jr.

She was owned by Russell Dize at the time of the Maryland Historical Trust Inventory. She had a round chine with fore-and-aft planking. In the 1988 Survey Fred Hecklinger recorded that Russell Dize, son of Dan Dize, worked her out of Tilghman Island since 1975. She was in excellent condition, and was a constant race winner. In 1993 we found her still in good condition and Russell Dize still the owner. *Russell Dize sold her to Harold 'Stoney' Whitelock at Deal Island in 2007 or 2008, and restoration was begun at Chance, Maryland. In 2011 she struck a buoy in the Deal Island race and nearly sank. She and her yawl boat were found to have much rot. Capt. Whitelock began a new rebuild, with the help of Coastal Heritage Alliance. She was located at Deal Island in 2015.*

Kathryn. Chesapeake Appreciation Days Skipjack Race. 1994.

- *Lady Katie* -

BUILDER:	YEAR:	SITE:
Bronza Parks	1955-56	Wingate, MD

LENGTH:	BEAM WIDTH:	DEPTH:	NET REG. WT.:
46.2' at water line 49' 5" on deck	16.2'	3.3'	8 Tons

INCLUDED IN:
• MHT Inventory 1983: T-533 • 1988 Survey • 1993 Search

Bay Dredging License # 25. Osylee Lewis related that she was "first owned by Bronza and then Eugene Wheatley, Mac's brother [Malcolm Wheatley] owned her with George Powley when they first started out. When Gene died, George took over full ownership." In the 1983-84 Inventory she was owned by Stanley Larrimore of Tilghman Island. She was not accepted on the National Register due to her age. In the 1988 Survey she was still owned by Stanley Larrimore, was well maintained, and was a regular winner in the work boat races. She carried passengers for 8 years until 1986. President Reagan came aboard in 1984 to give a speech on the Bay and the environment. In 1993 we found her at Tilghman, still owned by Stanley Larrimore, and still in fairly good condition. There had been some work done on her in Baltimore at the Living Classroom and the Chesapeake Bay Maritime Museum, St. Michael's, Maryland. *She was working out of Cambridge in 2015.*

Lady Katie. **Tilghman Island, MD. November 1993.**

– *Lorraine Rose* –

BUILDER:	YEAR:	SITE:
C. H. Rice	1949	Reedville, VA

LENGTH:	BEAM WIDTH:	DEPTH:	GROSS REG. WT.:
44.3'	15.2'	3.8'	10 Tons

INCLUDED IN:
• MHT Inventory 1983: T-534 • 1988 Survey • 1993 Search

Bay Dredging License #9. Dan Dize recalled, "Elmer and Clyde Evans had her built over here ta Reedville. She was a right good dredge boat. Clyde and them made right good money into 'er. We used the term, she was 'right stiff' ya know [resisted heeling]. She carried more sail accordin' ta the average boat 'er size."She did not qualify for the National Register due to her age. In 1988 Fred Hecklinger related that Clyde Evans worked her until she sank at Annapolis. She was taken to Buck Garvin's dock at Tilghman, where Garvin bought repaired her and returned her to work. By 1988 she was laid up in the marsh and abandoned at Knapp's Narrows, Tilghman Island. We found her on 7/20/1993 dead in the water at Tilghman, totally rotted beside another derelict *Ralph T. Webster.*

Lorraine Rose. Ralph T. Webster in the background.
Tilghman Island, MD. July 1993.

- *Maggie Lee* -

BUILDER:	YEAR:	SITE:
---	1903	Pocomoke City, MD

LENGTH:	BEAM WIDTH:	DEPTH:	REG. WT.:
51.0'	16.0'	3.8'	Net: 8 Tons Gross: 10 Tons

INCLUDED IN:

• MHT Inventory 1983: T-535 • 1985 National Register p 68, #865 ref: 85001091,
• 1988 Survey • 1993 Search

Built with a rounded chine, the last of the Pocomoke Round Bottom dredge boats. She was owned by Robert Joshua Parks in the 1930's. Osylee Lewis remembered that she had been owned by Lloyd Kervin after he owned *Reliance*. Dave Faulkner added that she was Dan Dize's fifth boat, after he owned *Martha Lewis*. "She was built just like her." The Coast Guard appropriated her in World War II to look for submarines. In the 1988 Survey she was found to be severely hogged, with much rot, and in advanced deterioration. Her owner was Buddy Harrison, Tilghman Island. She was then at the Calvert Maritime Museum, Solomon's Island and Fred Hecklinger recorded that she "was not in condition to work this year. She had been sold to Baltimore, got in bad shape, and was bought back by Bill Bradshaw." She was restored in 1990 by Bunky Chance, who was her owner when she was seen in Oxford, Maryland in 1993. She was in bad shape, had been fiber-glased, was out of the water and was slightly hogged. She had fore-and-aft planking. *Her address in 2015 was West Denton, Maryland, at the Old Harford Town Maritime Center.*

- *Mamie Mister* -

BUILDER:	YEAR:	SITE:
---	1911	Champ or Deal Island, MD

LENGTH:	BEAM WIDTH:	DEPTH:	REG. WT.:
56.0'	18.4'	4.8'	Net: 19 Tons Gross: 24 Tons

INCLUDED IN:

Owned by Capt. Elbert Gladden and rebuilt in 1955 at Krentz boatyard. A bug-eye with two masts and three sails, she was taken to New York Harbor in 1980 where she was used for charters and sail training. Dredged 1991-1993 as a 3-sail bateau. When seen on 7/20/93 she was owned by D. K. Bond at Tilghman Island. She appeared outwardly sound. *In 2015 her address was Tilghman Island.*

ABOVE: *Maggie Lee.* Oxford, MD. July 1993.

BELOW: *Thomas W. Clyde* and *Mamie Mister*, bugeye. Dogwood Harbor, Tilghman Island, MD. July 1993.

- *Martha Lewis* -

BUILDER:	YEAR:	SITE:
Bronza Parks	1955	Wingate, MD

LENGTH:	MOLDED BEAM WIDTH:	DEPTH:	REG. WT.:
46' 3" at water line 49' 5" on deck	16' 7"	3.8'	Net: 8 Tons (long tons) Gross: 10 Tons

INCLUDED IN:
• MHT Inventory 1983: T-536 • 1985 National Register p 68, #865 ref: 85001091,
• 1988 Survey • 1993 Search • 2008 HA-2189

Bay Dredging License #8. She was not included in National Register due to age. In the 1988 Survey, Fred Hecklinger noted that she had a new after cabin in 1987, a raked mast 10 degrees, owners Gene and Etheldene Tyler of Tilghman Island. She was kept in "excellent condition," and did not sail as well as her sister boat *Lady Katie.* In 1993 we recorded that she required "some deck repairs" and was for sale. (This turned out to be an enormous understatement.)

- *Mary W. Somers* -

BUILDER:	YEAR:	SITE:
William Thomas Young	1904	Mearsville or Parksley, VA

LENGTH:	BEAM WIDTH:	DEPTH:	NET REG. WT.:
41.9'	14.0'	3.5'	---

INCLUDED IN:
• 1976 National Register p 31, #388 ref: 76002173 • 1988 Survey • 1993 Search

Built for Lloyd and Mary Somers, she was not examined in the 1983-84 Inventory, which was intended as an application for the National Register, likely because she was already on the Register since 10/8/1976. When registered her owner was Raymond Hartjen, of Educational Alternatives, Inc., in Port Tobacco, Maryland. In the 1988 Survey it was noted that she had been owned by 8 oystermen, had been at Ladenburg School, Piney Point, Maryland, and then at Port Tobacco. She was in "very bad shape." In 1993 she was found under a tarp on land at the Havre de Grace Maritime Museum. She was totally ruined and would require a complete rebuild.

Martha Lewis.

Mary W. Somers. Havre de Grace Maritime Museum. July 1993.
Courtesy Allen Rawl.

- *Minnie V.* -

BUILDER:	YEAR:	SITE:
John Ventra	1906	Wenona, MD

LENGTH:	BEAM WIDTH:	DEPTH:	REG. WT.:
45.3'	15.7'	3.0'	Net: 8 Tons Gross: 10 Tons

INCLUDED IN:
• MHT Inventory 1983: T-537 • 1985 National Register p 68, #860
• 1988 Survey • 1993 Search

Bay Dredging License #50. Dan Dize reminisced that "Charlie Middleton owned her here on Smith Island. And when he retired, his son, Willie Middleton, took her over. After that Leonard and Roland Evans, two brothers, bought her and worked her here a long time. And then that's when they took her up to Baltimore to rebuild her." In 1983-84 she was owned by the City of Baltimore and leased to the Harrison Oyster Company, Tilghman Island. In the 1988 Survey Fred Hecklinger documented that she had been acquired by the City of Baltimore in the early 1970s. In approximately 1980 she was rotten, and Melbourne Smith (builder of the *Pride of Baltimore*) was commissioned to completely rebuild her in 1980-81 for the City. She was built in a manner to keep her documentation. *Anna McGarvey* was built at the same time using *Minnie V.'s* lines. *Minnie V.* worked in the winter under the direction of Buddy Harrison of Tilghman Island, and in the summer carried passengers for the Maryland Historical Society. In 1993 we found her still in Baltimore in good shape, with Capt. Robert (Bob) Keith still carrying passengers. *In 2007 she was listed as owned by the Living Classroom, and in 2015 she was still working in Baltimore.*

Minnie V. Fells Point, Baltimore, MD. July 1993. Courtesy Allen Rawl.

– *Nathan of Dorchester* –

Builder:	**Year:**	**Site:**
Bobby Ruark	1994	Cambridge, MD

Length:	**Beam Width:**	**Depth:**	**Net Reg. Wt.:**
45.0'	16.0'	---	---

Included In:

Not on the Maryland Historical Trust Inventory or on the National Register, since she was built by Bobby Ruark for the Cambridge Foundation, in Cambridge, Maryland. We visited her on 7/20/1993 while she was under construction, and she was solidly and well built. *Her construction was completed in 1994, she sailed in the Chesapeake Appreciation Days Race on 10/95, and was well maintained when seen in 2015.*

Nathan of Dorchester. Chesapeake Appreciation Days Race. 1994.

- *Nellie L. Byrd* -

BUILDER:	YEAR:	SITE:
---	1911	Cambridge, MD

LENGTH:	BEAM WIDTH:	DEPTH:	REG. WT.:
53.6'	16.7'	4.8'	Net: 18 Tons
			Gross: 22 Tons

INCLUDED IN:
• MHT Inventory 1983: T-538 • 1985 National Register p 68, #867 ref. #85001093
• 1988 Survey • 1993 Search

Bay Dredging License #28. She was owned for many years by William Todd of Cambridge. Dan Dize recalled, "the *Nellie Byrd* used to be owned ta Deal's Islan'. An' then Clifton Webster owned 'er, an' then Darryl Larrimore. He's the one had 'er rebuilt, done a lotta work on that thing. She oughta be in right good shape. An' she's thick, you know [thick hulled, sturdy]." She had been extensively rebuilt by Darryl Larrimore in 1984-86. The 1988 Survey found her in "terrible shape" for many years at Cambridge. Larrimore had actively raced this boat as well as *Elsworth*, and sold her to Bart Murphy, the present owner at Tilghman Island. In 1993 she was in Baltimore and had received a new bottom, per Capt. Wade Murphy. *In 2015 she was working at Tilghman.*

Nellie Byrd. Tilghman Island. September 1993.

- *Ralph T. Webster* -

BUILDER:	YEAR:	SITE:
Sylvester Muir	1905	Oriole, MD

LENGTH:	BEAM WIDTH:	DEPTH:	NET REG. WT.:
47.7'	15.3'	3.5'	8 Tons

INCLUDED IN:
• MHT Inventory 1983: T-539 • 1985 National Register ref. #85001094
• 1988 Survey • 1993 Search

Oyster dredge number unknown. Dan Dize recalled, ' she was here t' Smith Islan', and Elwood Johnson owned 'er. She was a right good drudger. An' then 'e sold 'er to a guy t' Ewell by the name of Leon Evans. He was a right good drudger too. Then she went Deal's Islan', an' [the owner's] name was Ralph Webster, same as the boat, an' then she was sold to Tilghman Islan'. I hear she's dead at Tilghman now. They said they had a job akeepin' 'er afloat at times. Her keel and keelson were twisted an' fluvvered, an' that made the difference in tryin' ta keep 'er afloat. I used her boom for *Martha Lewis*, and scarfed it." Osylee Lewis recalled her as one of larger and most responsive dredgers on the Bay. "She'd go right around."

In 1988 she was "worn out at Tilghman, laid up in the mud and abandoned at Knapps Narrows. Capt. John Wilson dredged her until he was 91 and Capt. William Berridge until nearly 80 years of age." When seen on 7/20/1993 she was lying dead in the mud beside *Lorraine Rose*.

Ralph T. Webster. Tilghman Island, MD. July 1993.

- Rebecca T. Ruark -

BUILDER:	YEAR:	SITE:
Moses Geoghagen	1886	Taylor's Island, MD

LENGTH:	BEAM WIDTH:	DEPTH:	NET REG. WT.:
47.3'	15.7'	3.7'	10 Tons

INCLUDED IN:
• MHT Inventory 1983 • 1985 National Register p 68 #869 ref. #85001095
• 1988 Survey • 1993 Search

Oyster dredge number 29. She was rebuilt as a skipjack in the 1920s. She was sailed by Emerson Todd as owner and captain through the 1980s. In 1983-84 she was recorded as round-bottomed, rigged as a skipjack, with fore-and-aft planking. She was originally built as a sloop with a gaff mainsail. In 1988 Fred Hecklinger recorded that she was acquired in 1984 by Capt. Wade H. Murphy, Jr. and was in a rotten and seriously weakened state. After working one season, she was taken to Deagle's Shipyard in Deltaville, Virginia for an extensive rebuild during 1986-87. She had all new frames and hull planking, and after returning to Tilghman, new clamps were fitted and 60% of the deck beams, and 90% of the planking were replaced. The after cabin was constructed of all new material. She now makes a rather handsome appearance, and is perhaps the fastest sailer in the dredge fleet." She was seen on 7/20/1993, appeared in quite good condition, and won the Deal Island race on 9/6/1993. *She became a National Historic Landmark on 7/31/03. Capt. Wadey Murphy continued to work her out of Tilghman Island in 2015.*

- Reliance -

BUILDER:	YEAR:	SITE:
---	1904	Fishing Creek, MD

LENGTH:	BEAM WIDTH:	DEPTH:	NET REG. WT.:
41.0'	14.3'	2.7'	---

INCLUDED IN:
• 1976 National Register p 30 #384 ref. #76001013 • 1988 Survey

When she was entered in the National Register of Historic Places on July 30, 1976, her owner was Peter Teeling of Annapolis, Maryland. She was once owned by Stanley Larrimore. The 1988 Survey said she had been sold as a yacht in 1977. In 1993 Wade Murphy said she had been bought by two boys at St. Mary's, and was nearly gone. She was not seen that year. Osylee Lewis said Lloyd Kirvin had her at one time, then he bought *Maggie Lee*, a larger boat.

Rebecca T. Ruark. Capt. Wade Murphy. Deal Island Race. September 1993.

- *Rosie Parks* -

Builder:	**Year:**	**Site:**
Bronza Parks	1955	Wingate, MD

Length:	**Beam Width:**	**Depth:**	**Net Reg. Wt.:**
46.2' at water line 49' 5" on deck	16.7'	3.3'	8 Tons

Included In:
• MHT Inventory 1983: T-522   • 1988 Survey   • 1993 Search

Sister ship to *Martha Lewis* and *Lady Katie*. Bay Dredging License #19. In the 1988 Survey Fred recorded that Orville Parks, brother of Bronza, was the unofficial 'admiral of the Chesapeake', and sailed *Rosie Parks* for 20 years until he retired in 1975 at age 79 after 68 years working on the water. He won most often at the Deal Island Races, and won 9 of the first 10 races at Chesapeake Appreciation Days at Sandy Point, Maryland, as well as the 1962 Solomon Island Race. Orville donated her in 1985 to the Chesapeake Bay Maritime Museum. In 1993 we found her at the Museum at St. Michaels, Maryland, in poor shape but floating at the dock. Osylee Lewis remembered his uncle's boat as the fastest of the sister ships. *She underwent a complete rebuild at the Chesapeake Maritime Museum, St. Michael's, Maryland, and appeared to be in excellent condition in St. Michael's harbor in 2015.*

- *Ruby G. Ford* -

Builder:	**Year:**	**Site:**
William Smith	1891	Fairmount, MD

Length:	**Beam Width:**	**Depth:**	**Net Reg. Wt.:**
45.0'	15.6'	2.6'	5 Tons

Included In:
• MHT Inventory 1983: T-541   • 1985 National Register p 68 #870 ref. #85001096
• 1988 Survey   • 1993 Search

Dan Dize remembered her as a good sailing boat, "if it blowed hard." She was "stiff, an' don't nobody know why. She would carry about 500 bushels of orsters, *Ruby Ford* would."In the 1988 Survey her owner was Bart Murphy of Tilghman, who also owned *Esther F.* She had been an excellent sailer, but sank in early 1988 and was still under water. We saw her on 7/20/93 at Severn Marina, Tilghman, on the land, and totally gone.

ABOVE: *Rosie Parks.* Chesapeake Bay Maritime Museum,
St. Michaels, MD. July 1993.

BELOW: *Ruby G. Ford.* Severn Marina, Tilghman Island, MD. July 1993.

- *Sea Gull* -

BUILDER:	YEAR:	SITE:
C. A. Dana	1924	Crisfield, MD

LENGTH:	BEAM WIDTH:	DEPTH:	REG. WT.:
46.6'	15.9'	4.3'	Net: 10 Tons Gross: 17 Tons

INCLUDED IN:

• MHT Inventory 1983: S-239 • 1985 National Register p 67 #852 ref. #85001078
• 1988 Survey • 1993 Search

Bay Dredging License #56. Her owner, when she was entered in the National Register, was Capt. George Thomas or Capt. Jessie Thomas of Deal Island. In 1993 Gordon Gladden reported her as dead and gone. She was not found that year. *She was abandoned or broken apart in 1993, and was reported rotting near Oriole, Maryland in 2008.*

- *Sigsbee* -

BUILDER:	YEAR:	SITE:
William A. Noble	1901	Deal Island, MD

LENGTH:	BEAM WIDTH:	DEPTH:	NET REG. WT.:
47.0'	15.8'	3.8'	8 Tons

INCLUDED IN:

• 1985 National Register p 68 #871 ref. #85001097 • 1988 Survey • 1993 Search

In 1988 Fred Hecklinger recorded that she had been purchased by Wade Murphy in 1963. She was sold to *Bay Magazine* and was working during their ownership, but they could not manage her and she was returned to Capt. Murphy. She was a dull sailer, but won the Deal Island Race in 1988 and had sailed in all Chesapeake Appreciation Days Races between 1965 and 1988. She sank during the Chesapeake Appreciation Days Race in 1990, was sold to the Lady Maryland Foundation, and was taken to Baltimore for repairs at the Living Classroom. She was broken apart in 1990 and completely rebuilt with original lines. As *Sigsbee II* she sailed in the Deal Island Race on 9/6/93. Her home port was Baltimore in 2015.

Sigsbee. Baltimore, MD at Living Classroom. July 1993.

- *Somerset* -

BUILDER:	YEAR:	SITE:
C. H. Rice	1949	Reedville, VA

LENGTH:	BEAM WIDTH:	DEPTH:	NET REG. WT.:
44.9'	15.7'	3.5'	9 Tons

INCLUDED IN:
• MHT Inventory 1983: S-240 • 1988 Survey • 1993 Search

Bay Dredging License #33. Built for Capt. Elbert W. Gladden. She did not receive National Register recognition due to her age in 1985. In 1988 she was berthed at Whitehaven on the Wicomico River, in "above average condition for a Deal Island boat." Walton Benton was owner and captain. In September 1993 she was docked at Whitehaven, was working as a dredge boat and Capt. Benton sailed her in the Deal Island Race. *She was one of the skipjacks restored at the Chesapeake Bay Maritime Museum, St. Michael's, Maryland, Capt. Walt Benton.*

- *Stanley Norman* -

BUILDER:	YEAR:	SITE:
Otis Lloyd	1902	Salisbury, MD

LENGTH:	BEAM WIDTH:	DEPTH:	REG. WT.: Net: 7 Tons Gross: 10 Tons
47.5'	16.0' or 15.3'	4.0'	

INCLUDED IN:
• MHT Inventory 1983: T-543 • 1985 National Register p 67 #860 ref. #85001086
• 1988 Survey • 1993 Search

Bay Dredging License #60. Osylee Lewis said, "She was Uncle Willis Windsor's boat." She was extensively rebuilt in 1976 when Ed Farley of Bozman, Maryland bought her in poor condition. In the 1988 survey she was in "excellent condition, with good workmanship," and was rigged to carry 35 passengers for summer charters and winter dredging. She carried students for the Chesapeake Bay Foundation. Ed Farley then gave her to the Chesapeake Bay Foundation and in 1993 she was said to be in Annapolis. Stanley Norman *participated in the Chesapeake Appreciation Days races in 10/94 and 10/95. Her home port in 2015 was listed as Annapolis.*

Somerset. Whitehaven, MD. October 1993.

- Susan May -

BUILDER:	YEAR:	SITE:
---	1901	Pocomoke, MD

LENGTH:	BEAM WIDTH:	DEPTH:	NET REG. WT.:
46.0'	15.9'	3.6'	10 Tons

INCLUDED IN:
• MHT Inventory 1983: S-241 • 1985 National Register p 67 ref. #85001083
• 1988 Survey • 1993 Search

Her hull was that of a sloop with fore-and-aft planking, like *Rebecca Ruark* and *Kathryn*. Dan Dize remembered, "She was a right good drudge boat. Two brothers owned her and the *Maggie Lee*, Clyde Benton and Clifton Benton. The younger Benton they called Junior, dredged the *C. W. Crockett.*" In 1988 her owner was Clifton Benton, but she had not been dredging for 3 years, was rotten and hogged, quite dead at Wenona, Deal Island. We saw her at a distance in 1993 at Wenona, up in the mud and disintegrating.

Susan May. Wenona, Deal Island, MD. July 1993.
Courtesy Allen Rawl.

- *Thomas W. Clyde* -

BUILDER:	YEAR:	SITE:
---	1911	Oriole, MD

LENGTH:	BEAM WIDTH:	DEPTH:	REG. WT.:
54.5'	18.0'	5.3'	Net: 21 Tons Gross: 27 Tons

INCLUDED IN:
• MHT Inventory 1983: S-242 • 1985 National Register p 67 #858 ref. #85001084
• 1988 Survey • 1993 Search

Bay Dredging License #39. One of the larger skipjacks, she was owned at the time of the National Register entry (6/15/1985) by Capt. Charles Abbott of Wenona, Maryland. She had been extensively rebuilt in the 1960s. In 1988 the owner was Charles Abbott II, who inherited her from his father who died in 1986. Fred Hecklinger remembered *Thomas Clyde* as a dull sailer. In his survey, he found her floating, but much deteriorated, deserving a complete rebuild. Charles Abbott II still owned her when we visited her in 1993, and found her much deteriorated at Wenona. Thomas Clyde *was one of the skipjacks restored at the Chesapeake Bay Maritime Museum, St. Michael's, Maryland, and won the Deal Island Race in 2007. Home port was Tilghman Island in 2015, owner Capt. Lawrence Murphy.*

Thomas Clyde. Wenona, Deal Island. November 1993.

- *Virginia W.* -

Builder:	**Year:**	**Site:**
Harrison Lewis	1904	Guilford, VA

Length:	**Beam Width:**	**Depth:**	**Net Reg. Wt.:**
37.5'	13.5'	3.3'	5 Tons Cargo Capacity

Included In:
• MHT Inventory 1983: T-544 • 1985 National Register #85001098
• 1988 Survey • 1993 Search

Bay Dredging License #12. She had herring-bone bottom planking. Dan Dize remembered her well: "She got a long record behind 'er. Irvin Evans used to own her and he was a good dredger. Then he died. John A. Vissage bought 'er. After John A. sold 'er to 'is son and Elmer Evans, they dredged 'er for years and years. I seen 'er up ta Kent Island at Merritt Marina. I don't know who owned 'er. Then she was bought back an' put on a railway there at Tilghman and rebuilt. It was a right good job of it, and she's back dredgin' again." In 1988 she belonged to Robert Marion Marshall, who had owned her for many years. She was extensively rebuilt in 1980-1981, and was found at Knapps Narrows, St. Michaels, Maryland in excellent condition. She looked "like new." Capt. Bob Marshall still maintained her in good condition at Tilghman Island when we visited in July, 1993. *In 2015 her home port was Kinsale, Virginia, at the Port Kinsale Foundation, Capt. Marty Miller. She was bought in 2015 by Capt. Phillip Todd of Cambridge, Maryland, and returned to dredging. She won the 2015 Deal Island Race.*

Virginia W. Tilghman Island, MD. July 1993.

- *Wilma Lee* -

BUILDER:	YEAR:	SITE:
Bronza Parks	1940	Wingate, MD

LENGTH:	BEAM WIDTH:	DEPTH:	GROSS REG. WT.:
46.8'	16.2'	4.5'	20 Tons

INCLUDED IN:
• MHT Inventory 1983: D-649 • 1988 Survey • 1993 Search

She was the first skipjack built by Bronza Parks. Osylee Lewis related that Ralph Ruark owned her after his uncle Asbury Lewis and uncle Orville Parks, both of whom had her built by Bronza Parks. She was found in the 1983-84 survey to be yacht-like in appearance, neat, and with a mast raked 15 degrees. In the 1988 Survey owned and operated by Ralph L. Ruark. She usually worked out of Cambridge, but in that year she was not active. She had a new boom, new waist planks, new logs, rudder, yawl boat and a finished cabin. Her mast was now plumb. In 1993 we found her outwardly in good shape, docked at the bridge at Tilghman Island. Darryl Larrimore previously had owned her and now Robby Wilson of Tilghman owned her and was dredging. *She was restored by Herb Cardin in 1994, and again in 2002, when she was donated to Okracoke Alive, Inc. She dredged in 2005-06. In 2014 she sustained Hurricane Arthur damage, and in 2015 her home was at the Okracoke Community Square Foundation Docks.*

Wilma Lee. October 1993.

Recreational Skipjacks

- *Barbara Batchelder* -

Builder:	Year:	Site:
Bronza Parks	1955	Wingate, MD

Length:	Beam Width:	Depth:	Net Reg. Wt.:
---	---	---	---

Included In:
• 1993 Search

Built as a skipjack yacht for Irénée duPont, at the same time as construction of *Martha Lewis*, *Lady Katie* and *Rosie Parks*. She was maintained by Ralph Ruark at Wingate, had a long cabin, and was used by the du Ponts on trips to the Caribbean. In good condition in 1993.

- *Champion Girl* -

Builder:	Year:	Site:
---	---	---

Length:	Beam Width:	Depth:	Net Reg. Wt.:
---	---	---	---

Included In:

In 1993 Julie Forbes owned this small, gem-like skipjack yacht which she maintained at Havre de Grace, Maryland.

- *Good Intent* -

Builder:	Year:	Site:
---	---	---

Length:	Beam Width:	Depth:	Net Reg. Wt.:
---	---	---	---

Included In:

Yacht built. Resided at Scott's Cove, Deal Island. Not seen.

- Ida May -

BUILDER:	YEAR:	SITE:

LENGTH:	BEAM WIDTH:	DEPTH:	GROSS REG. WT.:

INCLUDED IN:

Bugeye yacht.

Ida May. Bugeye yacht. Tilghman Island, MD. September 1993.

- *Lady Helen* -

BUILDER:	YEAR:	SITE:
Elmer & Doug Lowery	1987 or 1988	Tilghman Island, MD

LENGTH:	BEAM WIDTH:	DEPTH:	GROSS REG. WT.:
28.0'	9.9'	---	---

INCLUDED IN:

The Lowerys built *Lady Helen* as a skipjack yacht. She was in the Choptank Race in 2011, the Crisfield Race in 2014, and sailed charters out of Rock Hall, Maryland in 2015.

════════════════════════════

- *Talbot Lady* -

BUILDER:	YEAR:	SITE:
---	1986	Skipton, MD

LENGTH:	BEAM WIDTH:	DEPTH:	NET REG. WT.:
48.0'	18.0'	3.0'	14.3 Tons

INCLUDED IN:
• 1993 Search

Built as a yacht, not a work boat and owned by A. P. Quimby, she was seen at the end of the dock at Knapps Narrows Marina, Tilghman Island in 1993. She sailed in the Chesapeake Appreciation Days race in 10/94. Her home port was Canton, New Jersey in 2015.

Talbot Lady. Skipjack yacht. Tilghman Island. September 1993.

Appendix C

A Genealogy of Wingate's Families

The intertwining of families in Wingate is a natural result of its relative isolation in earlier days, and is not atypical for Bayside populations in general. Because *Martha Lewis* was the product of this particular community, her pedigree is really the story of the people who created her.

I was most fortunate to have the help of several women who grew up in Wingate and continue to hold the keys to Wingate history. I am especially grateful to Mary Parks Harding (MPH in the family trees that follow), Gail Sterling Joubert (GSJ), Louise Sterling (LS), Kitty Lewis (KL), and Dorothy Ann Lewis Shortall (DS). Through them I was able to identify portions of Wingate family trees that pertain to *Martha Lewis* and her "sister" boats. Appendix B is an attempt at providing an orientation to the families and individuals mentioned in Chapters 2 and 3. For practical reasons, this outline is limited to individuals most directly related to this one particular skipjack, but with full understanding that all Wingate families contain scores of watermen and their descendants who are important to the culture and circumstances that produced *Martha Lewis*. Where available I have included mini-biographies, but these do meager justice to the rich lives of the people themselves.

Family lore is murky prior to the late 19th Century. The earliest Dean immigrants from England settled at East New Market in Dorchester County and later on Lower Hoopers Island. In the 19th Century some Deans owned large plantations. Their first known waterman was Whittington Dean, Jr., born c. 1830, and thereafter a large number of Deans were watermen.

James Matthew Lewis, Sr. from Hooper's Island was the first Lewis to come to Wingate, in 1885.

The first Parks immigrant from England was said to be a member of the House of Burgesses in Jamestown, and was later in charge of harvesting salt for the Colony. From then on, the Parks' migration took them to Accomack County, Virginia, and then in the 18th Century to the Chesapeake Bay islands, including Smith, Pone (Adams), Hoopers, Bloodsworth and Hollands Islands. They came to Bishop's Head and Wingate in the mid-19th Century.

The Todds were plantation owners in the 18th and 19th Centuries. Michael Todd (c. 1651-1730) was the first Todd in Dorchester County, in 1790. Their first waterman was Jabez Todd (1809 -1902), listed as a sailor in the 1850 census.

Interwoven through these histories, are the names of other early settlers from the British Isles: Bloodsworth, Powley, Windsor, Pritchett, Wheatley, Ruark, Woodland, and Moore.

The Dean Family

1 Whittington Dean, Sr. (c. 1793 – pre-1844)

   m. 1813 Mary Hurst (c. 1800 – post-1870) (GSJ)

   Whittington and Mary had 10 children, including:

      2 Charles Dean (1825 Hoopers Island – 1905 Hoopers Island)

        m. 1850 Patty A. Ruark (1828 Hoopers Island – 1910 Hoopers Island) Charles and Patty had 7 children, including:

          3 William H. Dean (c. 1853 Hoopers Island - 17 Dec 1904, in hunting accident)

            m. 1873 Mary Jane Lewis (1854 Hoopers Island -1964 Toddville → **Lewis 2**) (GSJ) William was a waterman.

      2 Whittington Dean, Jr. (c. 1827 Hoopers Island - 1910 Wingate)

        m. 1854 Mary L. Parks (c. 1830 Hollands Island - 1902 Bishop's Head → **Parks 2**)

        Whittington Dean, Jr. was the first Dean waterman. (LS, GSJ)

        Whittington, Jr. and Mary had 10 children, including:

          3 Whittington T. "Millard" Dean (1858 Hoopers Island – 1923)

            m. Zipporah Parks (1865 Hoopers Island -) (GSJ)

            4 Charles Whittington Dean (1894 – 1970)

              m. 1915 Maysie Tall (1893 – 1982)

              Charles worked for Cambridge Shipbuilding. (GSJ)

                5 Thomas Goldsborough Dean (1919 Wingate – 2002 Cambridge)

                  m. 1939 Clara Willey (d. 2002 Cambridge)

                Tom worked with Bronza Parks. (GSJ)

          3 Martha Miranda Dean (Dec 1862 - 16 Aug 1905, bur. Tom Powley's place, Wingate)

            m. 19 Aug 1885 in Crapo to James Matthew Lewis, Sr. (22 Jan 1864 Hoopers Island - 13 Sep 1937 Wingate → **Lewis 2**)

            Martha is the namesake for skipjack *Martha Lewis*. (KL, LS, GSJ)

          3 Charles S. Dean (1864 Hoopers Island - 1938)

            m. 1890 Carrie Lewis (1870 Hoopers Island – 1942 → **Lewis 2**)

THE LEWIS FAMILY

1 Matthew Kane Lewis (1827 Hoopers Island - 1905 Hoopers Island)
> m. 1853 Nancy C. Slacum (1827 Taylor's Island - 1909 Hoopers Island)
> Nancy was the daughter of George Slacum and Mary Todd)
> Matthew was a waterman. (LS, GSJ)
> Matthew and Nancy had 6 children, including:

2 Mary Jane Lewis (1854 Hoopers Island - 1946 Toddville)
> m. 1873 William H. Dean (c. 1853 Hoopers Island - 1904 → **Dean 4**) (LS, GSJ)
> William died in a hunting accident.

2 Carrie Lewis (1870 Hoopers Island - 1942)
> m. 1890 Charles S. Dean (1864 Hoopers Island–1938 → **Dean 3**)
> Charles was the brother of Martha Miranda Dean Lewis. (GSJ)

2 James Matthew Lewis, Sr. (22 Jan 1864 Hoopers Island - 13 Sep 1937 Wingate;
> m. 19 Aug 1885 in Crapo to Martha Miranda Dean (1862 - 16 Oct 1905 Wingate, → **Dean 3**)
> James was a waterman, a dredger, and later worked in Baltimore. He was the first Lewis to settle in Wingate, at the time of his marriage. He was buried at Tom Powley's place in Wingate, behind the church. (LS, GSJ)
> James and Martha had 8 children, including:

3 Asbury Morgan Lewis (1889 Wingate - 1962 Wingate)
> m. 1914 Lena "Lenie" Pritchett (1891 Wingate - 1973 Wingate)
> Lena is sister of Bertha Pritchett Powley (→ **Bloodsworth/ Powley 4**) and Anna Pritchett Parks (→ **Parks 4**).
> Asbury was a dredger and owned one-half of skipjack *Wilma Lee* with his brother-in-law Orville Parks. (KL, GSJ)

3 Willie Osgood Lewis (1894 Wingate - 1975 Hoopers Island)
> m. Lola E. Hooper (b. 1899 Hoopers Island)
> Willie was a waterman and had a crab house with brother-in-law Bronza Parks. Bronza built a draketail workboat for him in 1934, now at the Chesapeake Bay Maritime Museum,

called *Martha* after his mother, Martha Miranda Dean Lewis. (GSJ)

3 James Matthew Lewis, Jr. (13 Feb. 1889 Wingate – 15 Jul 1964 Cambridge; see also chapter 3)

>*m.* 1907 Floy Armenia Windsor (22 Feb 1891 Wingate - 11 Nov 1958 Wingate → **Windsor 3**)
>
>James was a farmer, then a waterman. He owned bugeye *Clarence and Eva,* skipjack *Sister* and workboats *Edna* and *Audrey.* He commissioned his brother-in-law Bronza Parks to build skipjack *Martha Lewis.* James is buried at Dorchester Memorial Park, Cambridge. (LS, GSJ)
>
>James and Floy had 10 children, including:

4 Norris Lewis (1913 Wingate - 2004 Cambridge)

>*m.* 1934 Eastland Moore (1915 Wingate - 2008).
>
>Norris and Eastland lived in Bishop's Head, where Norris was a waterman, and owned skipjacks *Elsworth* and *Mistake.* He had a seafood transport company named Lewis Seafood Express. (LS, GSJ)
>
>Norris and Eastland had 4 children including:
>
>>5 Dorothy Ann Lewis Shortall (contributor "DS" in this work)

4 Weller R. "Will" Lewis (1915 Wingate - 1970 Hoopers Island)

>*m.* 1937 Lillian Virginia Woodland [1916 Applegarth (Lower Hoopers Island) - 2009 Hoopers Island]
>
>Weller co-owned the *Sterling* and *Stewart Brothers* buy boats, and skipjack *Mishap* with his brother, Leon. They also owned a bait company at Hoopersville.

4 Osylee Lewis (22 Sep 1922 Wingate – 5 Jan 2012 Seaford, DE)

>*m. c.* 1944 Arie Naomi Parks (19 Apr 1924 Wingate - 6 Apr 2015 → **Parks 3**; *see also chapter 3*)
>
>Osylee was a waterman and he and Naomi had a crab pot manufacturing business. In later years he worked for Sears.
>
>>5 Jim Lewis
>>
>>>6 Dan Lewis
>>
>>5 Anna Lewis (1946-)

4 Leon Edmond Lewis, Sr. (1920 Wingate - 1997 Hoopers Island)

m. Rosa "Rosie" Elizabeth Parks [1923 Applegarth (Lower Hoopers Island) - 2013 Hoopers Island].

Leon co-owned *Sterling* and *Stewart Brothers* buy boats, skipjack *Mishap*, and a bait company with brother Weller. He also owned the buy boat *Agnes Elizabeth*, named for a daughter who died young. (AL, GSJ)

Leon and Rosa had 4 children, including:

5 Lemuel Stephen Lewis, Sr. (1950 -)

> *m.* Janet Spicer
>
> Lemuel survived workboat explosion October 1962.

5 Leon "Bud" Lewis, Jr. (Hoopersville)

> Bud was a waterman He died in a workboat explosion in October 1962.

4 Earl Jerome Lewis (1917 Wingate - drowned 1962)

> *m.* 1) Flora Parks (1923 Hoopers Island - 1949 Wingate)
>
> *m.* 2) c. 1950 Katherine "Kitty" Morris (1916 – 2000)
>
> Earl was a State Highway Patrol lieutenant and owned one-half of skipjack *Martha Lewis* with his father, James Lewis, Jr.

4 Edna Lewis (1911 Wingate - 2015 Taveres, FL)

> *m.* 1930 Malcolm Otis "Mac" Wheatley (1910 Wingate - 1988 Wingate)
>
> Malcolm was brother to Eugene Wheatley and son of Jabez Wheatley. He owned skipjack *Kathryn* and workboats *Edna W.* and *Valmarjon*. They donated part of their property to the Lakes and Straits Fire Department. (LS, MPH, GSJ)

4 David L. Lewis (1908 Wingate - 1983 Wingate)

> *m.* 1933 Mildred Gore (1915 - 2001)
>
> David was a waterman and consigned the skipjack *H. M. Krentz* in 1955 in Virginia. He owned buyboat *Bertie H.*, and three separate workboats, each named *Clara Anne*, after his daughter. (DS, LS, GSJ)

3 Nancy Lewis (1892-1980)

> *m.* 1) Merritt S. Moore (1890 - 1934 Bishop's Head), a waterman
>
> *m.* 2) 1943 Winnie M. Todd (1884 - 1960 Bishop's Head), a waterman and farmer. (GSJ)

Nancy and Merritt had 7 children, five of them watermen or watermen's wives.

3 Iva "Ivy" Lewis (1897 Wingate - 1993 Wingate)

m. 1919 Ebben McGlaughlin (1895 Bishop's Head - 1951 Wingate)

Ebben was a waterman and WWI veteran. (LS, GSJ)

Iva and Ebben had 4 children, including:

4 Norma McGlaughlin (1921 Wingate - 1979)

m. 1937 Marvin J. Simmons (1915 Hoopers Island - 1971)

Marvin was a waterman.

4 William James "Bill Tuck" McGlaughlin (1923 - 2007)

m. Aileen Ruark.

William was a waterman, worked with Bronza Parks, and was a WWII veteran.

3 Katie Thelma Lewis, (17 Sep 1899 Wingate - 8 Jan 1986 Glen Burnie)

m. 4 Sep 1918 Bronza M. Parks (20 Jan 1900 Wingate - 13 May 1958 Wingate → **Parks 5**)

Bronza was a renowned boat builder. He named one of his skipjacks *Lady Katie* after Katie Thelma.

THE PARKS FAMILY

1 William A. Parks (1801 Hollands Island - 1884 Wingate)

    m. Amelia Bloodsworth (1807 Hollands Island - 1880 Wingate → **Bloodsworth 2**)

    William owned property on Bloodsworth, Pone (Adams) and Hollands Islands. (GSJ)

    William and Amelia had 8 children, including:

  2 Mary L. Parks (c. 1830 - 1902 Bishop's Head)

    m. 1854 Whittington Dean, Jr. (c. 1827 - 1910 Wingate → **Dean 2**) (GSJ)

  2 Rebecca Frances Parks (1850-1925 Hollands Island)

    m. Capt. Robert John Wesley Powley (1884-1919 Hollands Island → **Bloodsworth 3**)

  2 Williamina Louisa Parks (1843 Hollands Island - 1924)

    m. 1864 waterman James Robert Wesley Adams (1840 Bishop's Head - 1909 Bishop's Head → **Windsor 2**) (GSJ)

  2 Jesse Thomas Parks, Sr. (1846 Hollands Island - 1912 Wingate)

    m. 1865 Margaret Jane Powley (1847 Hollands Island - 1923 Wingate, → **Bloodsworth/Powley 3**)

    Jesse was always a waterman and built some boats (DS, GSJ)

    Jesse and Margaret had 11 children, including:

   3 Albert Poole Parks (1878 Bloodsworth Island - 1954 Wingate)

    m. 1898 Octavia Gertrude "Gertie" "Aunt Tay" Tall (1876-1968)

    Albert was a waterman and builder. (GSJ)

   3 Lasbury Parks, Sr. (1880 Bloodsworth Island - 1965)

    m. 1903 Willie Arieanna Woodland (1889 - 1978)

    Lasbury was a waterman.

    Lasbury and Willie had 2 children:

    4 Mary Jane Parks (1920 - 2005)

      m. waterman Milton Dean (1904 - 1982)

    4 Naomi Arie Parks (19 Apr 1924 Wingate – 6 Apr 2015)

      m. Osylee Lewis (22 Sep 1922 Wingate – 5 Jan 2012 Seaford, DE → **Lewis 4**)

3 Peter Carol Parks (1885 Wingate - post-1940)

    m. 1910 Ruby N. Willey (c. 1895 - post-1940)

    Peter sold his property to nephew Bronza Parks for his boathouse and yard, and moved to Cambridge. (GSJ)

3 Robert William Wesley Parks (1873 Hollands Island - 1929 Pocomoke, MD)

    m. 1) Rosina "Rosie" Todd (c. 1877 Wingate - 1902 Wingate → **Todd 4**). Rosina is the namesake for the skipjack *Rosie Parks*.

    Robert and Rosina had 4 children (see below).

    m. 2) 1903 Laura "Lollie" C. Dean (1880 Wingate - 1966 Cambridge). Robert and Laura had 5 girls, 3 of whom married watermen. Robert W. W. owned the skipjack *Ida May* pre-1929. He was a waterman and farmer, and owned 201 acres in Wingate named "Parks Meadow." He was a police boat commander. In later years he moved to Cambridge. He died when his car was struck by a train near Pocomoke City, MD (GSJ, MPH)

    Robert and Rosie's children include:

4 Bronza Malone Parks (20 Jan 1900 Wingate - 13 May 1958 Wingate; *see also chapter 2*)

    m. 4 Sep 1918 Katie Thelma Lewis "Lady Katie"(17 Sep 1899 Wingate - 8 Jan 1986 Glen Burnie, MD → **Lewis 3**)

    Bronza was a renowned boat builder. He named one of his skipjacks *Lady Katie* for Katie Thelma. (GSJ)

    Bronza and Katie had 5 daughters:

5 Lucille Calena Parks (1920 Wingate - 2012 Merritt Island, FL)

    m. 1943 in Mariana, Fla. to Eugene "Gene" Bertram Sterling, (1930 Crisfield, MD -)

    Lucille was a teacher and Eugene is an Air Force retired Major General and pilot.

    Lucille and Gene had 3 children, including:

6 Gail Ann Sterling Joubert (1951-),

    Gail retired as a USAF Major and lives in Florida. She is family historian GJS in this record.

5 Irene Geneva Parks (1922 Wingate – 2011 Aiken, SC)

    m. Leonard "Andy" G. Anderson (1919 Kansas – 2015 Aiken, SC)

5 Martha Rosetta Parks, twin of Mary Rosina Parks (1927-)

    m. 1) Ralph Ruark (1923 - 2002) who owned skipjack *Wilma Lee* (built by Bronza Parks 1940)

    m. 2) George Todd, insurance agent in Cambridge, MD.

5 Mary Rosina Parks, twin of Martha Rosetta (1927 Wingate -) (MPH)

    m. 1946 Warren Preston "Pres" Harding.

5 Joyce Estella Parks (b. 1932)

4 Orville Hilson Parks (1896 Wingate - 1976 Cambridge),

    m. 1919 Wilsie Pritchett (1900 - 1979).

    Orville served in WWI in France, worked on the water all his life. He owned skipjack *Wilma Lee* with brother-in-law Asbury Lewis. *Wilma Lee* was named for one of Orville's daughters and for Asbury's granddaughter, Barbara Lee, daughter of Thomas and Evelyn Lewis Foxwell. Orville owned skipjacks *Ida May*, *Joy Parks* (which he named for his daughter Joy), and *Rosie Parks* (named for his mother) which he donated to the Chesapeake Bay Maritime Museum. (GSJ, MPH)

    Orville and Wilsie had 4 children, including:

5 Joy Parks, youngest child, b. c. 1933, namesake of skipjack *Joy Parks*. (MPH)

5 Wilma Parks (c. 1927 -)

    m. _____Willey. Namesake of skipjack *Wilma Lee*. (GSJ)

4 Robert Joshua "Robbie" Parks (1897 Wingate - 1964 Cambridge)

    m. 1916 Anna "Annie" Pritchett (1900 Wingate - 1991). Anna is sister of Bertha Pritchett Powley (→ **Bloodsworth / Powley 4** and Lena Pritchett Lewis (→ **Lewis 3**). Robert was a farmer, then a waterman, had a dredge boat, built a "stone house" in Wingate used as a restaurant then tavern (GSJ).

Robert and Annie had 8 children, including:

5 Calvert O'Neill "Cody" Parks (1939-2007)

   m. 1947 Nancy Lee Holliday (1929 - 2007)

   Cody worked on the water and at Bronza Parks' and Jim Richardson's boat yards. Owned *Dorothy Lee*, one of Bronza Parks' boats. (MPH, GSJ)

5 Marvin Parks (1922 - 2012 Crapo),

   m. 1946 Doris Travers (- 2005).

   Marvin was a waterman and worked at Bronza Parks' and Jim Richardson's boatyards. He was a WWII veteran and piloted a mechanized landing craft. (GSJ)

THE TODD FAMILY

1 Thomas McIntyre Todd (c. 1781 – before 1822)
    m. 1807 Priscilla Willin (c. 1781 -) (GSJ)
  2 Thomas S. Todd (1814 – 1889)
    m. Amelia "Millie" Todd (1816 – 1885)
    Thomas and Amelia had 8 children, including: (GSJ)
    3 James Edward Todd (1844 – 1922 Crocheron)
        m. 1867 Sarah Catherine Powley (1850 Hollands Island –
        1925 → **Bloodsworth/Powley 4**) (GSJ)
    3 John Major Todd (1851 Bishop's Head – 1935 Wingate)
        m. 1871 Sydney A. Powley (1852 Hollands Island – 1935 →
        Bloodsworth/Powley 4)
        John and Sydney had 9 children, including: (GSJ)
      4 James E. Todd (1874 – after 1940 Cambridge)
          m. Hannah E. E. Todd (1874 Bishop's Head – 1947
          Cambridge)
          Hannah is daughter of Richard Q. and Leah Todd, be-
          low. (GSJ)
  2 Jabez Todd (1809 – 1892)
    m. Baltimore to Hannah Anne Wheatley (1820 – 1900).
    Jabez was a sailor, then a farmer.
    Jabez and Hannah had 11 children, including: (GSJ)
    3 Richard Q. Todd (1850 – 1923 Bishop's Head)
        m. 1) Leah A. (1851 – 1893 Bishop's Head), who bore all of
        Richard's 6 children, including, below.
        m. 2) 1896 Angeline E. "Annie" (1853 – 1925). (GSJ)
      4 Hannah E. E. Todd (1874 Bishop's Head – 1947 Cambridge)
          m. 1898 James E. Todd (1874 – after 1940 Bishop's
          Head)
          James was a waterman. See above.
      4 Rosina "Rosie" Todd (c. 1877 Wingate – 1902 Wingate)
          m. Robert William Wesley Parks (1873 Hollands Is-
          land – 1929 → **Parks 3**) (MPH, GSJ)

The Bloodsworth/Powley Families

1 Robert Bloodsworth, Jr. (c. 1774 Somerset County, MD - 1843)

    m. 1807 Margaret "Peggy" Wingate

2 Amelia Bloodsworth (1807 Hollands Island - 1880 Wingate),

        m. William A. Parks (1801 Hollands Island - 1884 Wingate → **Parks 1**) (GSJ)

2 Nancy Ann Bloodsworth (1815 Hollands Island - 1899 Bishop's Head)

        m. 1843 Nicholas Powley (1806 Hollands Island - 1862)

        Nicholas was a waterman and sailor. (GSJ)

3 Risdon Powley (c. 1842 Hollands Island -1888)

        m. Elizabeth Dail (c. 1855 – unk.)

4 Thomas Risdon Powley (1878 – 1967)

        m. Archie Jones (1884 – 1966)

        Archie is the daughter of Charles H. Jones and Mary E. Dean Jones. → **Dean 3**

3 Robert John Wesley Powley (1844 Hollands Island – 1919)

        m. 1868 Rebecca Frances Parks (1850 Hollands Island – 1925 → **Parks 2**)

4 Risdon Asbury Powley (c. 1877 – c. 1962)

        m. 1909 Bertha "Berthie" Lou Pritchett (1889 – 1977)

        Risdon was a waterman.

        Bertha is the sister of Lena "Lenie" Pritchett Lewis → **Lewis 3** and Anna "Annie" Pritchett Parks. → **Parks 4**

5 Robert Edward "Bobby" Powley (1916 Wingate – 1993 Eldorado, MD)

        m. Marion Windsor (1927 Wingate – 2014 Eldorado, MD)

3 Margaret Jane Powley (1847 Hollands Island - 1923 Wingate)

        m. 1865 Jessie Thomas Parks, Sr. (1846 Hollands Island - 1912 Wingate → **Parks 2**)

        Jessie was always a waterman (GSJ), built some boats. (MPH, GSJ, DS)

4 Sarah C. Powley (1850 Hollands Island – 1925,

> > *m.* waterman James E. Todd (1844 – 1922 Crocheron
> > → **Todd 3**)

> **4** Sydney A. Powley (1852 Hollands Island – 1935 Wingate)
> > *m.* 1871 waterman John Major Todd (1851 Bishop's
> > Head – 1935 Wingate → **Todd 3**) (GSJ)

Bibliography

Berry, David (2008) *Maryland's Skipjacks*, Mount Pleasant, SC: Arcadia Publishing.

Blackistone, Mick (2001) *Dancing with the Tide: Watermen of the Chesapeake*, Atglen, PA: Tidewater Publishers.

Blackistone, Mick and Parker, James (1988) *Sunup to Sundown: Watermen of the Chesapeake*, Santa Barbara, CA: Acropolis Books.

Bradley, Wendell P. (1969) *They Live by the Wind*, New York, NY: Alfred A. Knopf.

Brewington, Marion V. (1963). *Chesapeake Bay Log Canoes and Bugeyes*, Schiffer Publishing, (December 1).

Burgess, Robert H. (1965) *Chesapeake Circle*, Atglen, PA: Tidewater Publishers.

Burgess, Robert H. (1963) *This Was Chesapeake Bay*, Atglen, PA: Cornell Maritime Press.

Chapelle, Howard I. (1998) *Notes on the Chesapeake Skipjacks*, St. Michaels, MD: Chesapeake Bay Maritime Museum

Cooper, Dick (2010) "Saving the Rosie Parks" in *Bay Journal* Chestertown, MD (November 17).

Cooper, Dick (2011) "The Birthplace of Rosie Parks" in *The Chesapeake Log*, (Fall)

Cooper, Dick (2011) "Two Worlds Collide: The Murder of Bronza Parks," *Talbot Spy*, www.talbotspy.org (November, Avalon Foundation).

Cooper, Dick (2013) "Voices from the Past: Stories from Bronza Parks' Boatyard," *The Chesapeake Log*, St. Michaels, MD: Chesapeake Bay Maritime Museum (Winter/Spring).

Dean Family Association of Dorchester County (1940), *Deans of Dorchester*, Dorchester County, MD (January).

De Gast, Robert (1970), *Oystermen of the Chesapeake*, Camden, ME: International Marine Publishing.

"Dragging of River Continues for State Police Officer," *Cecil Whig*, Elkton, MD 1962.

Evans, Ben (1982) "Survivor Recalls Tragedy on Choptank River," in Salisbury, MD: *Daily Times* (July 4).

Jacoby, Mark (author) and Greer, Jack R. (editor) (1991) *Working the Chesapeake: Watermen on the Bay*. University of Maryland Sea Grant Publications (January 1).

Lawson, Glenn (1988) *The Last Waterman*, Crisfield, MD: Crisfield Publishing Company.

Lewis, Effie Young (1995) *Tom Young's Skipjacks*, Delmar, DE: Evans-Coates Printing.

Lewis, Robert J.C.K. (2009), *Lewis Patriarchs of Early Virginia and Maryland, 3rd edition*, Berwyn Heights, MD: Heritage Books.

Maryland Historical Trust (1988), *The Maryland Skipjack Fleet: A Model Preservation Plan*, Annapolis, MD: Maryland Historical Trust.

Maryland Historical Trust (1985), "National Register of Historic Places Inventory – Nomination Form: Chesapeake Bay Skipjack Fleet."

Skipjack (1973), Volume 1: 1 Cambridge, MD: Students of South Dorchester High School

Vojtech, Pat (1993), *Chesapeake Bay Skipjacks*, Atglen, PA: Tidewater Publishers.

White, Christopher (2009), *Skipjack: The Story of America's Last Sailing Oytermen*, New York, NY: St. Martin's Press [Amazon lists Lanham, MD: Rowman and Littlefield Publishers]

"Third Annual Skipjack Sail Leaves Wenona for Crisfield" *Somerset Herald* (October 6, 1992)

Truitt, Reginald V. (1968) *High Winds, High Tides: A Chronicle of Maryland's Coastal Hurricanes*. University of Maryland Natural Resources Institute.

Index

CPSIA information can be obtained
at www.ICGtesting.com
Printed in the USA
LVHW07s0051050718
582674LV00020B/464/P